Black Matters: Lewis Morrow Plays

T0246279

Black Matters: Lewis Morrow Plays

Baybra's Tulips
Begetters
Mother/son

Edited by
NICOLE HODGES PERSLEY

methuen | drama
LONDON • NEW YORK • OXFORD • NEW DELHI • SYDNEY

METHUEN DRAMA
Bloomsbury Publishing Plc
50 Bedford Square, London, WC1B 3DP, UK
1385 Broadway, New York, NY 10018, USA
29 Earlsfort Terrace, Dublin 2, Ireland

BLOOMSBURY, METHUEN DRAMA and the Methuen Drama logo are trademarks of
Bloomsbury Publishing Plc

First published in Great Britain 2022

Foreword © Lewis Morrow, 2022
Introduction © Nicole Hodges Persley, 2022
Baybra's Tulips © Lewis Morrow, 2022
Begetters © Lewis Morrow, 2022
Mother/son © Lewis Morrow, 2022

Cover design by Rebecca Heselton
Cover image: *Homage to Quindaro* by Glen Walters

A catalogue record for this book is available from the British Library.

Library of Congress Cataloging-in-Publication Data

Names: Morrow, Lewis, author. | Hodges Persley, Nicole, 1969- editor. | Morrow, Lewis. Baybra
tulips. | Morrow, Lewis. Begetters. | Morrow, Lewis. Mother/son.
Title: Black matters : Lewis Morrow plays / Lewis Morrrow ; edited by Nicole Hodges Persley.
Description: London ; New York : Methuen Drama 2022. | Identifiers: LCCN 2022005382 (print) |
LCCN 2022005383 (ebook) | ISBN 9781350289727 (hardback) | ISBN 9781350289710 (paperback)
| ISBN 9781350289734 (epub) | ISBN 9781350289741 (pdf) | ISBN 9781350289758 (ebook)
Subjects: LCSH: African Americans–Drama. | LCGFT: Drama.
Classification: LCC PS3613.O77852 B58 2022 (print) | LCC PS3613.O77852 (ebook) |
DDC 812/.6—dc23/eng/20220408
LC record available at https://lccn.loc.gov/2022005382
LC ebook record available at https://lccn.loc.gov/2022005383

ISBN: HB: 978-1-3502-8972-7
       PB: 978-1-3502-8971-0
       ePDF: 978-1-3502-8974-1
       eBook: 978-1-3502-8973-4

Typeset by RefineCatch Limited, Bungay, Suffolk
Printed and bound in Great Britain

To find out more about our authors and books visit www.bloomsbury.com
and sign up for our newsletters.

For Anaya and Solomon, who have been the cause of no pain, only joy; no trauma, only peace. Daddy loves you.

Contents

Preface

Lewis Morrow

I love writing and it is the only passion I've had my entire life. I love Black people. Also, I love theater. Theater was a late discovery for me and as I found myself working a full-time job with two kids and having the audacity to pursue acting jobs, rehearsals, writing workshops, and development opportunities, I realized there is no way to *half-way* be an artist. I give this everything I have (I must acknowledge and thank my wife, Angela, because without her I couldn't have two kids, a full-time job, the audacity to be an artist, *and* effectively wear all those hats). I write plays from a place within me that feels these stories must be told. I believe that is the inherent arrogance all artists must possess—that what they create is worthy of others' attention. Yet, not for accolades, attention, nor money, but I write because I love writing and I love theater. Which is peculiar coming from where I'm from, as I find myself trying to give crash courses on what exactly theater is or at least alerting my people (Wyandotte County, Kansas) to its range which also exists in the gray between Shakespeare and gospel plays. When in the barber shop and wanting to gain support, it's not the easiest pitch—getting someone to commit their Friday evening to seeing a play. So, in the spirit of brevity, I found simply saying, "Ey, you know ya nigga wrote a play, huh?" generally suffices. Curiosity is a great fisherman. Yet, it is important to me that these brothers and sisters from the barbershops and salons, if no one else, are familiar with my work because I write for them. I write *for* whom I write about. Doing so was advice bestowed upon me by Mr. Harvey Williams, a man ten feet tall in my eyes who advised me early on to keep one thing at the forefront of my mind as I write—telling the story I want to tell the way I want to tell it. Otherwise, what is it all for? That is why I wrote these three plays, which in my mind I knew would be a trilogy from the first line I typed in the winter of 2018—when I started *Baybra's Tulips*. I wanted to write three plays that didn't center Black Lives Matters but instead Black life. I didn't want to educate non-Black people through these stories, but instead embolden Black people. This is us, Black people, as we try to figure things out amongst ourselves.

Often, by those who have either read my work or attended a production, I'm asked, sometimes light-heartedly, sometimes desperately but always in earnest, why do I write *tragic* things. My instinct is to admit that I've tried my hand at comedy and I'm of no use to anyone in that capacity. That would be true. Yet, what is also true—and most true I might add—is I am moved by the tragic things in life because where there is tragedy there is triumph. There is redemption. There is resilience. There is an opportunity to reflect and seek something different for ourselves or for others after us. I offer tragedy and everything that comes with it, the subsequent sadness, unexpected even if inappropriate and much–needed humor, discoveries, and growth, while thanking those who offer their own brand of storytelling because without one another there would be no reason for all of us to exist. Light only is because there is darkness; a truism, yes, but how much of one thing does anyone actually need? All I can offer as a story, expecting others to find it of substance, is what I also find of substance. In short, these are the stories that come to me, that stick to me, that I cannot shake and feel as though they must be put into words. Rest assured, when something funny sticks to me, I'll write it the best I can and hope that it is worthwhile to someone.

Introduction

Nicole Hodges Persley

Black Matters: Lewis Morrow Plays: Baybra's Tulips; Begetters; Mother/son is an anthology that maps the impact of emotional, social, cultural, and economic forces that shape the quality of Black life in the twenty-first century in the United States on Black terms of engagement. Morrow writes stories of dreams deferred, lives incarcerated, and families broken by circumstance through characters who are Black without apology. Bending time to create hyperreal poetic engagements that disrupt linear narratives, Morrow's elevated prose and reverence for Black vernacular speech as it is lived, spoken, and felt in everyday Black lives mirrors the experiences of what it *feels* like to *be* Black. The urgency and poetics of minute-to-minute decisions that shape how Black people live reverberate in the dialogue of his plays. His plays matter because he believes that the mattering of Black life is something that is done twenty-four hours a day, seven days a week, 365 days a year. His works profess that Blackness is something that is active, in motion, in a constant state of being and becoming that is as infinite and regenerative as the cosmos themselves. Being Black, for Morrow, cannot be contained in the colloquialisms of a hashtag. This statement is not to dismiss the #Black Lives Matter movement on any level. Quite the contrary. Morrow's trilogy asks something of us as a community—a global Black community. He dares us to be who we are—free and able to accept ourselves the way that we are—to seek light in the gray areas of our lives that tether between morality and poetry, deviance and excellence, freedom and unfreedom, love and apathy.

I am writing this introduction right at the end of the world premiere of *Baybra's Tulips,* the first play in this trilogy, at KC Melting Pot Theatre in Kansas City in September 2021. I have the pleasure of working with Lewis Morrow as a director of his plays, as a collaborator, and as the Artistic Director of KC Melting Pot Theatre, founded by the inimitable Harvey Williams, a Black theater visionary who opened the door for many artists, including myself. I remember running to Harvey Williams to tell him how special this play was and that we had to produce it at KCMPT. In *Baybra's Tulips*, siblings Baybra and Tellulah test the boundaries of sibling love as they stand in the rubble of their childhood memories. Released from prison after ten years, Baybra returns to his sister's home to reconcile his relationship with her and to challenge suspected spousal abuse by his brother-in-law Charles. As Baybra attempts to piece the fragments of his life back together, we see how Black families navigate the trauma of the present as they strive to break the generational curses of the past. During the run of the show, I watched audiences on the edge of their seats grappling with the contradictory emotions that this play brings to the surface. Directing *Baybra's Tulips* was a career highlight and a special moment for the KCMPT family.

I am inspired by the visceral quality of Morrow's writing. His urgent tone places the sins of living smack in the middle of the play, giving audiences no escape. The past and the present are always connected in his works. Creating an ideological remix that echoes the work of W. E. B. Du Bois, Booker T. Washington, and Malcolm X, Morrow's prescriptive ethos challenges Black people to focus on themselves and to disregard imposed stereotypes and tropes. Morrow forces us to look in the mirror and to face what we see, like it or not. The Black family is not just a nuclear relationship, nor a responsibility that is met through the provision of food, water, shelter, and tough love. He asks us to explore the cultural and emotional inheritances that we leave from one generation of Black people to the next and to step up to a higher version of ourselves.

In the second play of the trilogy, *Begetters*, we see such complex conversations of generational inheritance as we meet Norma and Spicer, a couple in their twilight years who are forced to face the toxic effects of their marriage on their adult children, Gordon and Andrea. A seemingly mainstream trope of the happy marriage becomes a complex interrogation of the thin line between love and hate within the Black family. Morrow asks, if we measure success in marriage by years together, and survival as evidence of life, what do we lose by not wanting and expecting more? *Begetters* challenges us to be better and to do better by the ones we love. The play's premiere production at KC Melting Pot was directed by Ile Haggins in May 2022.

The last play of the trilogy, *Mother/son*, is a powerful story of truth telling and the price we pay to tell it. John tries to save his mother Lydia from herself as she struggles with a drug addiction that has plagued their family for the most part of his and his sister's lives. He invites his mother to get sober at his home, offering her one last shot at redemption. Confronting his mother's whiteness, her privilege, and the aftermath of her behavior on their family, John must decide if his love for his mother will allow him to forgive her faults, and the pain that she caused him, which are now part of the infrastructure of who he is. The play premieres at KC Melting Pot in September 2022. It is my hope that this trilogy will afford many directors, actors, casts, and audiences around the world the opportunity to experience Morrow's devastatingly beautiful portraits of Black life that tell it exactly like it is with no apology, excuses, or explanation. Black people have and always will matter.

Baybra's Tulips

Baybra's Tulips received its world premiere on September 17, 2021, at KC Melting Pot Theatre in Kansas City, Missouri with the following cast:

Baybra	Lewis Morrow
Tellulah	Jabrelle Flournoy
Charles	George Forbes
Vanessa	Markeyta L. Young
Vince	Donald Paul Jones, III
Avery	Anaya Morrow

Director	Nicole Hodges Persley
Set Design	Doug Schroeder
Lighting Design	Doug Schroeder
Sound Design	Dennis Jackson
Costume Design	Lynn King
Dramaturg	Melonnie Walker
Stage Manager	Theodore "Priest" Hughes
Assistant Stage Manager	Desmond "337" Jones

Characters

Baybra *(bay-brə), Black man*
Tellulah, *Black woman*
Charles, *Black man*
Vanessa, *Black woman*
Vince, *Black man*
Avery, *Black girl, pre-teen*

Setting

Charles and Tellulah's kitchen

Time

Circa 2018.

Slash (/) indicates overlapping dialogue and where the next line should begin.
Ellipsis (. . .) indicates searching for words or weighted silence.

The Black characters are speaking in Black vernacular—not to be confused with illiteracy or lack of education. For the most part, words aren't misspelled to indicate this. If an actor is struggling with this, they've probably been miscast.

Act One

Scene One

Charles *returns home from work. He enters through the back door in the kitchen which is customary; the front door is used for strangers. His home is a family home passed down to him and it has a good mix of character and newness. It has a pantry, a nice size island, a kitchen table, and a doorway leading to the rest of the home. There's something cool about the way Charles walks and talks—a deacon now but he's got a sly past. He's charming and it works on most folks. He's a man of fifty or so and depending on the moment he can seem older or younger than this. On this evening,* **Charles** *comes home and takes a seat, but not before grabbing a carton of orange juice out the fridge and a cigarette. He lights up the cigarette and takes a puff. Then he opens the orange juice and takes a big swig, never noticing* **Baybra** *lurking in the shadows.*

Baybra   Still drinking shit straight out the carton, huh?

Charles (*startled*)   Hot damn! What the . . . Baybra? You scared the shit out of me.

Baybra   Brother Charles. *Deacon* Brother Charles.

Charles *hasn't seen* **Baybra** *in a long time. He's taking him in; more excited to see* **Baybra** *than* **Baybra** *is to see him.*

Charles   Boy look at 'cha! I can't believe what I'm seeing! Man get over here. Good to see you, baby brother.

They embrace, **Baybra** *unenthusiastically.*

Charles   You put on some weight, boy. Solid too! Your sister showed me some pictures but they don't do you justice. What the hell you been eating?

Baybra   Boiled eggs. Ramen. Tuna. You know, bullshit mostly.

Charles   You been throwing some iron around too, ain't 'cha? Looking like a bull. What you benching? Three hundred? Three-twenty-five?

Baybra   Give or take.

Charles   I've been doing a lot of yoga myself.

Baybra   Yeah? That's cute for an ol' nigga like you.

Charles *squeezes out a laugh.*

Charles   Same ol' Baybra. (*Beat.*) So, you got out a little early, I see. Your sister wasn't expecting you til next week.

Baybra   Too many niggas and too few cells, I guess. They woke me up this morning and said get dressed and get out and I told them motherfuckers yes sir. Ain't ask no questions.

Charles   You should've called us. We could've picked you up and did a little something special for you.

Baybra   I didn't want to put you all out the way. Vince picked me up and drove me around some.

Charles   You hungry? I grilled some chicken last night. Still got some left. Let me heat it up for you.

Baybra   Nah, I'm good. I'm giving up meat.

Charles   Giving up meat? Don't look like you gave up meat.

Baybra   Well, I didn't give it up in there but I told myself once I got out I'd give it up.

Charles   Oh, oh, oh, I see. This was twelve hours ago you gave it up. Gotcha. (*Beat.*) You know your sister gonna want to cook for you. Not no vegetarian mess either. Something down home and hearty. She was planning on having a bunch of folks over the house next week to welcome you back. We just gonna have to move it up to this weekend.

Baybra   Yeah, well that's exactly what I don't want. I don't want to see folks jumping out the damn closet trying to surprise me like they're excited I'm home.

Charles   People just missed you, Baybra. That's all.

Baybra   Shit. What people? My sister missed me. Vince, Vanessa. I'm praying my baby girl did too. You know, the only ones who came and saw me, who wrote me— they can claim they missed me. Nobody else. (*Beat.*) Not even you, Charles.

Charles   I asked about you all the time. Every time your sister talked to you or went to see you. I just didn't know if you wanted to see me to be honest. I mean : . . with everything that happened . . . you know . . . I just /

Baybra   Yeah, it's cool. Speaking of *everything*, how are you and Tellulah doing?

Charles   We're doing real good, Baybra.

Baybra   Real good, huh?

Charles   We hit our stride. I ain't had a drink in years. I'm only smoking one, maybe two of these cancer sticks a day. Going to give them up too. Going to church regularly. I'm telling you man, we've been good. Truly.

Baybra   Well, congratulations.

Charles   And you know I run the stores now. Yeah, my daddy left all of them to me and business been good. I've expanded it; we got three locations now. Turns out people still love a corner store where you can grab a burger or a gallon of milk all hours of the day. I'm thinking you may just be the guy I need to help me run 'em. Whichever one you run, we can add your name to the sign and everything—*Charles and Baybra's One Stop*. Don't worry about getting no job. I got you.

Baybra   Nah, I'll find something.

Charles   Why you wanna go work for peanuts? You in the circus or something? Cause you sure ain't in a cage no more.

Baybra   . . .

Charles   Listen, all I'm saying is you gonna need some real money in your pocket. A place to stay. Stability. That's what me and Tellulah here for. To help you get on your feet. It ain't a handout. It's what family is for.

Baybra   Am I family though?

Charles   Of course you are. Why would you say that?

Baybra   I don't know. I heard some things through the grapevine whereas if I was family I feel like I would've heard them directly.

Charles   Things like what?

Baybra   Nothing we gotta talk about now. Shit'll float to the surface sooner or later.

Charles   Alright, I guess. You brought it up, not me.

Baybra   So uh, Vanessa and Avery, you've been looking out for them, is that right?

Charles   You know I do. They come over for dinner at least three times a week. Vanessa and your sister out now. Catching a movie. Avery is with your mama. But they're always over here.

Baybra   How she looking?

Charles   Avery? Tall. Pretty as all get out.

Baybra   Nigga, I know what my daughter looks like. I got a thousand pictures. I'm talking about Vanessa.

Charles   How she looking or how she doing?

Baybra   You know . . . she looking like she doing alright?

Charles   I thought she came to see you.

Baybra   She came and saw me a few times early on but said she didn't like seeing me that way. So she didn't come much after that. They wrote me every other week though. That was even better to tell the truth. I ain't want them to see me that way. But I'm sure you knew that already.

Charles   Yeah, I might've heard them talking. I like to let their business stay their business though. I don't meddle. (*Beat.*) She don't have no man, you know.

Baybra   I ain't ask all that. I just asked how she was doing.

Charles   You actually asked how she looked. And she looks good. You going to try and pick things back up?

Baybra   . . .

Charles   I get it. Probably too soon to think about all that. So . . . you uh . . . what you going to do now that you're out? Anything planned?

Baybra   You don't have to do that, Charles. We spoke. Did the whole song and dance. I wasn't trying to interrupt your evening routine of orange juice and cigarettes. I was just hoping I could surprise my sister.

Charles   Hey, you don't have to tell me that your sister is who you here for. I'm just an . . . *accessory*. I get that. But I'd like to talk to you too. I missed you, Baybra. I know you said I don't get to say that but I'm going to say it because it's true. And I'm glad you're here. It makes things whole again.

Baybra   So I told you not to say it but you gonna say it anyways? Oh what, because it's your house? You say what you want?

Charles   Nah, it ain't like that, Baybra.

Baybra   I know it ain't like that. I ain't that same little nigga looking up to you, Charles. I don't look up to nothing but God . . . if that. I might just look Him in His eyes too.

Charles   I understand. I didn't mean no disrespect.

Baybra   Listen, what time you think Tellulah'll be back?

Charles   Anytime now. Make yourself at home. She already got the guest bed ready. I'm sure it'll break her heart if you don't stick around here at least a few days.

Baybra   You know I ain't in the business of breaking anything on my sister. So sure, I'll stay. A little while.

He begins to exit to another room.

Charles   Baybra . . . I didn't come see you cause I knew I wouldn't be able to convince you that I changed with that glass wall between us. I was hoping to shake your hand. To hug you. Let you feel it—that I was a different man now. I believe I was able to show your old man before he passed. Vanessa can see the difference. And your sister, you know, she the one who count. And she'll tell you I do right by her. I know you've been worrying and wasn't no peace of mind to be had. She could tell you things were good but it ain't the same as being here and seeing it yourself. I want you to know, things are good around here. See, I gave my heart to Jesus, man. I told Him, *it's your real estate, Lord. It's your house. But if you don't mind I want my wife to have the biggest room because I need to make things right with her.* And God done brought us a long way. Everything that went down, I don't know what that was or who I was, but I ain't him no more.

Baybra   So, I ain't the same ol' Baybra and you ain't the same ol' Charles. Is that right?

Charles   I don't even know who that old Charles was. But he's gone, Baybra. I swear to you. (*Beat.*) I killed that motherfucker.

Baybra   Well, see, that's good to know. I was hoping I ain't have to get out and kill that nigga myself. Because the *new Baybra* would. (*Beat.*) He'd break his motherfucking neck.

Scene Two

Baybra, **Charles**, **Tellulah**, **Vanessa**, *and* **Avery** *sit around after having dinner.* **Charles** *is picking up plates and taking them to the sink.*

Charles   Dinner was good, baby. *If you are obedient, you will eat the good things of the land.* I must've been better than good today.

He winks at and caresses his wife.

Vanessa   Go ahead and get the Tupperware ready because I'm taking some of this home.

Charles   Nah ain't no to-go plates, sweetheart.

Tellulah   Besides you don't ever bring our Tupperware back. Where's my good bowl with the lid that locks?

Vanessa   Heffa' I brought all that back.

Tellulah   Go ahead and get you a paper plate and put some foil over it. That's all we got for you.

Vanessa   You gonna let her do me like that, Charles?

Charles   Ey, I want some of these leftovers myself.

Vanessa   Well, give me Baybra's then. He's just sitting over there eating a can of green beans.

Baybra   I damn near ate all that cheesy-garlic bread. With all that . . . cheese and—and—and . . .

Tellulah   Garlic?

Baybra   Right. See I liked the way you browned the asiago and burnt the shit out of the crust.

Tellulah   Ah, man, shut the hell up. It was toasted perfectly.

Vanessa   Explain to us again, Baybra, why are you eating like this?

Baybra   I'm on some new cerebral shit. So I gotta feed the body differently so I can feed the mind and spirit differently.

Charles   *Man cannot live off bread alone!* Feed that soul first. Feed it right and you'll be just fine. My mama use to say don't ever forget you gotta soul.

Avery   Grandma says none of us *have* a soul. She said we *are* a soul and we have a body.

Charles   I guess my mama stands corrected.

Avery   But I do think you're right.

Vanessa   Who?

Avery (*indicating* **Baybra**)   Him.

Baybra   *Him*? I guess I ain't daddy to you then, huh?

Avery   You are. I guess it just seems funny. I never had to say it until now.

Baybra   *Never had to say it?* You never talked about me?

Avery   I did.

Vanessa   She did.

Baybra   Well, what you call me when you needed folks to know who you were talking about?

Aver   *Him.*

Vanessa   Anyways, baby girl, what were you saying?

Avery   Just, I suppose Daddy's right. If I go to school hungry, or church, I can't focus. But when I eat good, I can pay attention. You have to take care of that first.

Baybra   She's got sense. That's for sure.

Vanessa   She's got sense as long as she's saying you're right.

Baybra   Hell yeah, that too.

Charles   You ain't going to be able to go cold turkey, boy. I'll tell you that now.

Vanessa   He's been eating something. Look at him. He got rid of that bird chest somehow.

Baybra   Oh, so you like what you see, huh?

Vanessa   I mean, I'm impressed. Had you looked like this a few years ago you might've gotten a few more visits.

Charles   / You ain't right, Vanessa!

Tellulah   Girl!

Vanessa   I'm just saying . . .

Baybra   But you ain't saying much.

Avery   Daddy, question, do you have to give up meat completely or could you just eat it in moderation? Grandma and Grandpa Tony says everything is okay in moderation. Well, not everything. Grandpa Tony said—and I quote—*some shit you can't even do a little.*

Vanessa   Avery!

Avery   That's what Grandpa Tony said, Mama. But like gummy bears, I love gummy bears, those things are good intermittently.

Baybra   Who is this kid? *In moderation. I suppose. Intermittently.* Why don't you just talk like a little kid?

Avery   What, *goo goo gah gah?* I used to talk like that all the time. You just weren't around . . . Daddy.

Vanessa   Avery!

Baybra   Nah, she's alright. She can say that. Ain't nothing but the truth. (*To* **Avery**.) See, I ain't like your Grandma or Grandpa Tony with that old head mentality, where you supposed to respect your elders no matter who they are or what they're about. I'm not going to demand a respect from you that I haven't earned just because of some label. And that's all "Daddy" is, it's just a label if you don't put nothing with it.

He gets in **Avery***'s face.*

Baybra   But if you wanna be Billy Badass and talk shit like you grown, which hey you can do, just know you might fuck around and get your feelings hurt, little girl. I ain't seen you like you ain't seen me; I can be numb to it all too. Now, why don't you take your little ass, grab some gummy bears since you love 'em so damn much, a juice box, and go color or something. Let the adults talk.

Avery *rolls her eyes and leaves. Everyone stares at* **Baybra**.

Baybra   What?

Tellulah *tries to ease the tension.*

Tellulah   Well, muscles or no muscles, Baybra ain't strong enough to keep rejecting my food. Tomorrow is chicken and sausage gumbo. And I'm not making no alternatives. I bet that'll break you.

Baybra   Aw nah, your little brother don't break. Can't break. You learn mental fortitude if nothing else when it's just you and four walls.

Charles   I know that's right.

Baybra   Do you now, deacon? You know, huh?

Charles   Well, I don't have no intention of finding out for myself if that's what you mean. I'm just taking your word for it.

Tellulah   Besides, my man doesn't have any business locked up in nobody's jail.

Charles   Tell him, baby.

Baybra   Charles' ass ain't got what it takes anyways.

Charles   Ey, fine by me. I ain't got what it takes to get shot in my back and still walk straight either. But backs weren't meant for bullets and men weren't meant for cages.

Baybra   Sometimes you gotta go through something to know how much you can take. I've been tried and tested. I made it off the line, baby. I'm ready for war.

Charles   Nah, you looking for war. I'm looking for peace. The best shot is the one you never have to take. The best punch is the one you never have to throw.

Baybra   The best punch is the one that knocks the other nigga out.

Charles   Black hands ain't meant to harm Black bodies, brother.

Baybra *is about to show him up big time.*

Baybra   Charles . . . I know / you ain't about to—

Tellulah   OKAY! We get it. You're both wise and profound.

Vanessa   Let them tell it. They were gonna go on and on, weren't they?

Baybra   Yeah, well, get back to washing those dishes then, brother Charles.

Vanessa   So, has it hit you that you're a free man? Starting to feel back at home yet?

Baybra   Nah. Because this isn't my home.

Tellulah   Yes it is!

Charles   Every inch of it's yours. And we mean that too.

Baybra   That's a nice gesture and all, but you see, if it was my home I could do as I please. Put my feet up on the coffee table. Walk around naked. Leave my shoes in the hallway. Or, take me a pretty little thing, like Vanessa here, upstairs to that master bedroom, in that king size bed and play buck naked Twister. Like the good ol' days.

Tellulah   Okay, okay, okay. We get it.

Baybra   Can I do that, Charles? Can I get that big ol' bed and you all take the couch?

Charles   Uh . . . hell no. Because me and your sister got business to tend to ourselves in the bed. Matter fact, if you hear that lock go *click click*, you might want to get ghost cause it's going to get real loud, you feel me?

Tellulah   Oh my God! Charles, why you have to try and beat him at his own game?

Charles   Hey, I'm just saying.

Vanessa   Might as well hand them two a ruler. May the best man win.

Baybra   Hell nah! The deacon's old, shriveled-up ass don't want that.

Charles   Oh come on now, son. All them weights you lifting don't help with what we talking about right now. What we talking about is God given and God's been good to me.

Baybra   Please. Sound like a nigga trying to overcompensate to me. Cause God and me both know you ain't ever lifted a weight a day in your life.

Charles   The only thing I gotta be able to lift is your sister. I pick her up and put it down. Don't I baby? I said I pick it up and put it down all night long!

Tellulah (*sarcastic as fuck*)   Oh yeah, mmm hmm. All night long, baby.

Baybra   That don't sound too convincing. (*To* **Vanessa**.) Me and you can do better than that, can't we?

Vanessa   How the hell did I get dragged into this?

Baybra   Cause you *purty* and I likes ya, baby.

Vanessa   Gee, thanks.

Tellulah   Baybra, what you going to do with a grown ass woman like Vanessa? It's been too long, baby brother. You sure you even know where to *put it*?

Baybra   Well, there's only so many places it can go, big sister.

Vanessa   Baybra will you shut up!

Tellulah   He gets his nasty ass sense of humor from Daddy.

Charles   Yeah he does. Now, your daddy could say some things that'd make a fifth street nigga . . .

They all give **Charles** *a look.*

I mean a brother . . . an ol' fifth street brother blush.

Baybra   He wasn't that bad.

Tellulah   He wasn't?

Charles   Don't get me wrong, he was funny. As long as he wasn't talking about you. Otherwise, his humor was an acquired taste.

Baybra   Yeah, I might've gotten a little bit of that in me.

Charles   You got more than just that. You got his temperament. His nose. His eyes. You came out looking just like him. Look like him now. Cortland Jr.! And *junior* ain't ever been more appropriate.

Tellulah   But see there, I saved you.

Baybra   How you save me?

Tellulah   I got everyone to call you Baby Brother.

Vanessa   That's right! Itty bitty baby brother.

Baybra   Alright, keep on, Vanessa. You gonna make me say some shit. (*To* **Tellulah**.) And what they call me is *Bay-bra* cause you couldn't say baby nor brother with your ol' non-talking ass.

Tellulah   So what, it's cute.

Baybra   What grown ass man wants a cute name?

Charles   I suppose the places you've been you don't want too many people calling you *baby* nothing.

Baybra   Damn straight. I let you all slide. Other folks better call me by name. Or if you see I'm in a bad mood call me the motherfucker you don't wanna fool with cause I'm quick to slap a bitch.

Tellulah   Come on, Baybra. You know Charles don't want that kinda talk in here.

Charles   It's alright, baby. I done heard worse. We just talking.

Baybra   That's right. Besides, he ain't no reverend is he? Cause I'll watch my mouth around a reverend. But a deacon? Shit, what's that mean to me?

Vanessa   Don't be an ass, Baybra.

Baybra   See! Look! Vanessa said ass.

Tellulah   I'm asking you to respect my husband's house. Now, if it was somebody besides you he would've checked them himself but he's letting you slide. I'm not going to.

Baybra   Oh so you checking me?

Playfully grabs his sister up.

Okay then, big sister, I apologize. Alright? Deacon Charles, please, forgive me. I'll say *by golly* and *gee willikers* from now on. Is that better?

Tellulah (*laughing*)   Go on, man! You get on my nerves. You get that from Daddy, too. Just saying whatever you want and trying to charm your way out of it.

Baybra (*not serious yet*)   And you get that from Mama. Telling me what I get from Daddy all the time and it's never anything good.

Tellulah   I always say good things about Daddy. Maybe you just haven't been around to hear it. I'm just saying, some of your ornerier ways you get from him and it doesn't take me or Mama to point it out.

Baybra (*he's dead serious now*)   Maybe we shouldn't be talking about his ornery ways. The man's dead. Let him rest in peace. If we're going to share memories, why can't they be the good ones?

Tellulah   As scarce as they were, huh? Dead beat fathers don't provide many warm fuzzies.

Charles   Whoa, hold on now, Baybra's right. I can't go along with that. I knew your daddy my whole life. He was a lot of things but a bad father he was not. That man loved his kids. Did for his kids. He was a damn good father.

Tellulah   No, see, you can say he was a good friend. A good co-worker. A good man. Or if you laid down with him, hell—you can say he was a good lover. But he wasn't no father to you. You can't say that.

Charles   Oh come on now. You in rare form. You showing out, ain't you?

Tellulah   All I'm saying is let a man's kids be the judge of how well he did or didn't do.

Baybra   Well, that means me. And I say he did just fine. Considering. Or are you forgetting about how he made sure we always had some money in our pocket? How we didn't want for anything. After Mama left him and got her a new man, how he was paying for that crippled ass nigga's bills too cause he didn't want to work.

Tellulah   He couldn't work! He was crippled! He had him a little check coming in though. Daddy wasn't paying his bills.

Baybra   Bullshit. If Mama didn't get some spending money for her and crippled Tony's ass, she acted out. She wouldn't let Pops pick us up. She wouldn't tell us he called. Nothing. But if he slid her something extra just for her, then he was her best friend.

Tellulah   If so, then she deserved it. He was a whore and a bum father.

Baybra   How you gonna say some shit like that, Tellulah?

Charles   Alright now, let's get back to laughing and talking and just . . . not this. Let's get away from this. Baybra's back home, everybody! Come on.

Tellulah   Fine by me, let's drop it.

Vanessa   So . . . um . . .did you all want to get together Friday for dinner? Me and Avery /

Baybra   Nah. Nah I ain't dropping nothing. I wondered when I'd get a chance to bring this up. I didn't want to come in starting shit /

Tellulah   / Like hell you didn't.

Baybra   But I don't like the way you all treated the old man. He laid up dying and you saw him less than you saw me. All he wanted was something good for all of you.

Tellulah   Is that what he told you, Baybra? While you and him were bonding? Him in assisted living and you a thousand miles away in prison? Neither one of you able to do shit for the other. Because truth be told, he didn't give a shit about you until Mama put his ass out. Then he decided to do something right. So maybe you should get on the phone and thank her.

Baybra   I ain't thanking her for shit! And-and-and-and I'll tell you what else, you don't need to sit here in front of Vanessa and Charles divulging family business.

Tellulah   My husband and the mother of your daughter doesn't qualify as family? Cause she's family to me. My girl twenty years strong.

Vanessa   For the record, there's no judgment from me. Me and your father were just fine Baybra. I loved him, Avery loved him and he loved us.

Baybra   Yeah, loved him so much you let Tony take his place. Avery ain't mentioned my daddy once but quick to say *Grandpa Tony* this and *Grandpa Tony* that. Y'all motherfuckers act like Tony saved us.

Vanessa   You should be glad Avery had people to fill gaps. Glad that everybody around that little girl wants best for her. Wants to pour into her. Tony included.

Baybra   Look here, don't preach to me about that nigga.

Vanessa   Then don't question me about him.

Baybra   I ain't questioned you.

Vanessa   If you questioning who I'm letting around my kid, you're questioning me and I'm telling you don't do it, goddammit.

Tellulah   See, this is Baybra for you. He wants to tell everybody how they're wrong and he's right. Doesn't matter that *he* was locked up ten years. Somehow, he's the most righteous amongst us all.

Baybra   I ain't said nothing about being righteous but I'm damn sure *right* and you wanna act like I'm not making any sense. All I'm saying is if you had a bone to pick with Pops, you had nothing but time and opportunity. But you waited til he got sick and let him die alone. That's how you dealt with it. But the man is dead now. You just want to keep counting his mistakes. He can't hear you no more, Tellulah. Shit, I bet you wasn't counting them up when he paid for your two college degrees just so you can be a housewife.

Charles   Come on now, Baybra. Tellulah handles all the books and the inventory for the business. Making sure everything is accounted for. She ain't no housewife.

Tellulah   We don't need to explain anything to him. Yes, Daddy paid for my college. So what? He had a financial obligation to us, Baybra. I'm not going to throw him a parade for owning up to that one expectation while missing the mark on every other one. *Crippled Tony* was at your basketball games. Driving you to tournaments. Taking me to the father–daughter dance.

Baybra   What the hell kind of dancing was he doing?! You know damn well you were embarrassed by his ass spinning around in that damn wheelchair.

Tellulah   Tony and his friends moved me into my dorm. Called to check on me every weekend. Tony was at your trial.

Baybra   Because Pops didn't want to see me go out like that! Tony didn't ever come visit me though, did he? Him or your no-good ass mama.

Charles   Hey, man! Watch your mouth. Don't talk about your mother like that.

Baybra   You had your mind made up about Pops. Mama won you over. She had me on her side too until I got old enough to see she wasn't some innocent victim. She was mean. She was cold. She was unaffectionate. She ended up getting what she needed most—a nigga who was dead from the waist down and a house with a ramp. That way she ain't even have to roll him around.

Tellulah   You disrespectful ass Black bastard!

Charles   Listen, calm down—both of you. Now, I knew your father. He was the big brother I never had and I / loved that man.

Baybra   You know what, Charles? This is between me and my sister. I don't want to hear how close you and my pops were. Yeah, you were like his little brother and as soon as Tellulah was barely legal you made your move, didn't you?

Charles   I was years behind your old man. Don't try to imply I'm some old damn pedophile.

Vanessa   Baybra, come on, stop. Drop this. We don't need to talk about any of these things right now.

Tellulah   We don't ever need to talk about it as far as I'm concerned. I can do as I damn well please. I didn't need Daddy's approval.

Baybra   Clearly. You both made choices. Fine. So have I. All I'm saying is he doesn't get to be the authority on my father and constantly try to tell me something about him.

Charles   I know we weren't on the best of terms, your father and me, but we /

Baybra (*abruptly*)   He hated you. Did you know that? He hated your ass, Charles. Up until the day he died. If it seemed any other way, it was only to stay close enough to keep an eye on you. But whatever love was there withered away, man. He hated you the moment you stepped to my sister. He hated you more when you married her. But he hated you most when you beat up on her and broke her damn jaw. And if he wouldn't have been sick and if he wouldn't have been too old, he would've broke every bone in your body, nigga, then dumped your ass in a river! And I would've been right there tying the bricks around your goddamn ankles!

Tellulah   Damn it! Get the fuck out of my house, Baybra!

Baybra (*patronizing*)   Whoa, you gonna talk like that in front of the good deacon? Not to mention your niece is in the next room.

Tellulah   That's right. My niece, *your* daughter. Why don't you go spend some time with her instead of running your mouth in here to me? First time seeing her in what, eight years? Afraid to look at her and, let me guess, just like Daddy's sorry ass you got somebody to blame for that.

Baybra   Damn right I do. Look how she looks at me. Like I'm an alien or something. You could've brought her to see me. Vanessa could've. Mama. None of y'all did. Talking 'bout you didn't want to see me that way. Wasn't no other way to see me.

Charles   Baybra, please, settle down, man.

Baybra   You could've too, Charles. Yeah, but I know why you didn't want to show your face. I'm surprised you got the audacity to stand here now looking at me. Talking about you a *new Charles*, all the while looking and sounding and smelling like the same no good ass nigga you always been.

Charles   Baybra, give me a chance at least. I can't show you nothing in two days.

Tellulah   Charles, stop kissing his ass! (*To* **Baybra**.) See, I knew you were going to come here talking shit. Disrupting things. Charles said *well if he does, let him. It'll be* *good to have him around.* (*To* **Charles**.) But you didn't owe him nothing. (*Back to* **Baybra**.) He don't owe you anything, Baybra. He paid for what he did. He owed me and he paid it. He made it right with Mama as a bonus. Him and Daddy ended on good terms too. All was forgiven. He's proven himself. Vanessa, you can serve as witness. Hasn't he changed? He has. Hasn't he?

Vanessa   Yeah, Tellulah. Of course.

Tellulah   But you want to come back as if you were the missing piece. Like he has to prove himself to you and then everything can be restored. But things were made right long before you came back, Baybra. You can accept that or you can leave but ain't nobody waiting around for you to say it's okay to move on with their lives.

She leaves the kitchen and **Charles** *follows behind her.* **Vanessa**, *tired of* **Baybra**, *is about to head out last but* **Baybra** *stops her.*

Baybra   Oh what, you're mad too?

Vanessa *still leaving the room.*

Baybra   Come on, Vanessa. Hold up.

Vanessa   I don't think so, Baybra. I just want to get Avery and go home.

Baybra   I need to talk to somebody.

Vanessa   Talk to a shrink.

Baybra   They ain't gonna have the answers I'm looking for.

Vanessa   Neither do I.

Baybra   Look, I don't trust him.

Vanessa   Who?

Baybra   . . .

Vanessa   Charles? Okay. Well, you don't trust him. That's on you, Baybra. You have to get over that.

Baybra   It wasn't that long ago you were telling me how Avery calling him Uncle Charles made you cringe. Now he's your best friend?

Vanessa   *Not that long ago?* It was years ago, Baybra. You're the only one who hasn't realized that. But it's been ten years. Things change.

Baybra   Do they?

Vanessa   What does that mean?

Baybra   I just want to know what you really feel about it. They act like everything is all gravy. It seems off to me. That's all I'm saying.

Vanessa   Baybra, listen to me, the window to figure all that out has closed. This conversation is pointless. That's why I stopped coming to see you. This is all you talked about. I was waving my hands, yelling at the top of my lungs, *Baybra! Hello!*

Do you see me? You see your daughter? But all you could talk about was Tellulah and Charles. Or who was doing your daddy wrong. How low-down your mama is. Avery was growing up, I was changing and you were just sitting there, stuck, stagnant, and content with that shit. After so long I stopped reading your letters. I'd just give you an update on Avery and sign a little smiley face. Hoping at some point you'd see everyone has moved on. Hoping after so long you would just move on.

Baybra   *Just move on.* That's a helluva luxury, *Ms. Free-to-do-what-you-like-the-past-ten-years.* Let me tell you something, where I was at, wasn't no *moving* and wasn't nothing *on.* Everything was stuck, broke, and off. So, excuse the hell out of me if I was in there thinking about some shit.

Vanessa   All I'm saying / is you—

Baybra   And see, you ain't the one who was burdened with the knowledge of what's really going on around here.

Vanessa   What the hell are you talking about?

Baybra   I'm talking about my old man having good reason to believe Charles never stopped beating on my sister. Yeah. Never. Tellulah was pregnant, too. Did you know that?

Vanessa   No . . . see . . . no. Shut up. You know how many doctor visits I've went on with Tellulah? How many times I held her while she cried her eyes out? Every doctor saying the same thing. She wants them. Charles wants them. Everyone wants them for her. But she just can't have kids. You know that shit yet you're listening to your father and why?

Baybra   No, it would be hard for her to have kids. Not impossible. And she got pregnant, Vanessa. But lost the baby . . . because of Charles.

Vanessa   If your sister was pregnant, she wouldn't have been able to go one minute without telling me. Who do you think you are? Popping up out of nowhere like you been here and I'm the one passing through. You got that twisted all in knots, baby.

Baybra   So my father was lying?

Vanessa   Baybra, what are you doing? You've been free two days and you're trying to carry out some plot devised by your father on his deathbed? This is your priority? Not building something between you and your daughter. Not getting back in school or finding something you're passionate about. Not even getting some ass or a date or just something. Instead you just want revenge?

Baybra   Are you saying my father was lying?

Vanessa   Your father was sick.

Baybra   And so what? The man could see. He could hear. He knew when some shit wasn't right. Not to mention he said my mother finally came around too. It was a gift if you will. He didn't have much longer and she confided in him that he was right about Charles after all. I guess Tellulah laid it all out there to my mama. And see, him telling me? That's for Tellulah. That's him saving Tellulah. Because he knew I wasn't about to sit by and watch it happen.

Vanessa   What don't you understand?! If any of this were true Tellulah would've told me! Not her mother. Not her father. Not you. Me!

Baybra   See, I believe Tellulah told Mama because she just needed someone to talk to and she knew my mother wouldn't confront her. My mama is weak like that. But if she brought it to you, you'd have said something. And when it comes to that nigga, Tellulah doesn't want to be told what's right, she just want to hear *she's* right. But I'm telling you, Vanessa, we've been left in the dark. You and me. The only ones she's ever had for real.

Vanessa   Have you talked to your mother about this?

Baybra   My mother would just deny it. But her and my father were weird like that. After forty years, a couple of kids and everything in between, they still talked about things. I know she told him. I believe that.

Vanessa   Listen to me, your father was on the outside looking in, Baybra. For the last few years he was alone. He was sick. And he was angry. I'm telling you what I know to be true. What I saw for myself. Then, with a frail body and scattered mind I believe he told you something knowing you would carry it on long after he was gone. He's trying to use you to disrupt things because he can't any longer. And you feel obligated to him because when he was sick you couldn't be there. And you feel obligated to Tellulah because when she needed you most, you weren't there for her either. But this person you're trying to be who fixes things and makes them good again isn't wanted around here. You need to just let it go. You need to figure out where you fit. Stop digging for shit. Otherwise, if you keep digging, you'll end up in a big hole by yourself wondering where all these skeletons are not realizing you're standing in your own grave.

Baybra   . . .

Vanessa   Okay. Whatever. So that's it? That's what you needed to talk to someone about?

Baybra   Nah, that's not it.

He begins to approach her. She evades.

I want to know if it's worth me trying to show you the good in me.

Vanessa   Baybra, you think I've been waiting around all this time hoping and wishing you were going to come back with something to offer me? All I was hoping was that you would in fact make it back and you could get a second shot with Avery. I took myself out of the equation when you got locked up in the first place.

Baybra   Well, I ain't take you out of it.

Vanessa   That doesn't matter.

Baybra   Sure it does.

Vanessa   What you wanna hear, Baybra? That I got a soft spot for you? Well, I can admit that. A part of me is asking what the hell is fate cooking up. I could've found someone else in all this time but I haven't. You could've . . . hell, you *should've* convinced yourself I was out of your reach but you didn't. Now we're standing in here, looking at each other like we don't have nowhere else to turn. But that's not the case. You and me, we've always needed something to keep us close. It used to be Tellulah. Now, it's Avery. But it's never been just us. So please don't misinterpret this. I'm standing here with you because I care about you. I believe you can be a great father. I've thought about you. And I just want you to be alright. But you don't need to show me anything. I don't have any stake in it. Show yourself. Show it to Avery.

Baybra (*he moves in again, she evades again*)   Avery looking to you to see what she's supposed to do. I gotta salvage you and me first. If she sees you trust me, she'll trust me.

Vanessa   It doesn't work that way, Baybra.

Baybra   If I wouldn't have gotten mixed up in some shit, where would we be? Huh? Don't you remember? I was coming around. I was blooming. Growing up. My head was on my shoulders . . . or almost. You becoming a possibility made me want to do right.

Vanessa   It didn't make you want to do right too damn bad.

Baybra   It makes me want to do right now. I just need to know doing right is going to be worth it.

Vanessa   It's always worth doing right, Baybra. Regardless of what you can get out of it. (*Beat.*) And how you gonna talk about wanting to do right? Look at how you were just acting with Charles and Tellulah.

Baybra   That's different. That's my sister. You can't expect me to just sit still if I think she's in trouble. I ain't letting her down again. So I'm going to get to the bottom of whatever is going on with them. (*Beat.*) And . . .

He touches her. She's stuck. He kisses her.

I'm going to get to the bottom of whatever is going on with us. Unless you saying I shouldn't go digging for that either. Is that what you saying?

Vanessa *finally gives up. They kiss and it escalates quickly. It's going down.*

Scene Three

A few days later. **Avery** *sits at the table writing.* **Charles** *enters kitchen from the living room. He wasn't expecting her to be there.*

Charles   Hey, baby girl.

Avery   Hey, Uncle Charles.

Charles   I didn't even know you were here.

Avery   Mama dropped me off so her and Aunt Tellulah could run some errands. You were napping so we just let you sleep.

Charles   I wasn't napping. I was dozing off.

Avery   Well, whatever it was. Your eyes were closed and you weren't moving. You're not dead so I thought you were sleeping.

Charles   Nah, I was just resting. You know, I'm glad it's just you and me. We need to hang out more.

Avery   Why?

Charles (*he's amused by her bluntness*)   Hell, I don't know. For sentimental reasons I guess. You hungry?

Avery   No, I'm okay.

Charles   What you drawing?

Avery   I'm writing.

Charles   What you writing?

Avery   Just some notes for a story.

Charles   What's it about?

Avery (*frustrated by the interrogation she closes her notebook*)   Nothing at all, Uncle Charles.

Charles   Oh, I'm sorry. Excuse me, Miss Lady. I wasn't trying to interrupt you.

Avery   Yet it happened, nonetheless.

Charles   Your daddy's right. You talk a lot of stuff. You need to hang around more kids.

Avery   I do. When I'm at school.

Charles   Yeah and then you're up under your mama or your grandma all day. (*Beat.*) That's how your daddy was though. Anytime he got the chance he was up under his old man. Made him think he was grown too. He'd say some of the damnedest things.

Avery   Hey, Uncle Charles, speaking of Daddy, can I ask you something? Why don't you two get along?

Charles   We get along alright.

Avery   I heard him yelling at you the other night.

Charles   Oh. Well, we could probably get along better. We used to. We used to be pretty tight. He won't tell you but he used to look up to me. I looked up to your Grandpa Cortland and your daddy looked up to me. I was sixteen when he was born. But we clicked. Yeah, that was my buddy. He'd listen to me. I could tell him things. If he lost his cool—because he had a temper on him, boy he'd go from zero to a hundred just like that—but I could tell him to calm down and he'd calm himself. He trusted me like that.

Avery   What happened?

Charles   Well, there's such a thing in this world as *losing credibility.* You know what credibility is?

She gives him a look; of course she knows.

Of course you know. Well, I lost credibility with your daddy. And rightfully so, I guess.

Avery   But why?

Charles   I was cursed, baby girl. I had the wrong daddy and the wrong things handed down to me. And I do things . . . or I did things, we all do things sometimes, that we watched others do and it ain't always right. That's about as well as I can put it.

Avery   So you messed up and Daddy didn't trust you anymore?

Charles   Yeah, I messed up and I didn't get the chance to fix it. Your daddy went to jail and we couldn't make it right. Too much time passed. Things needed attention, needed to be talked about, and instead we just let time go by. You can't go out there and break your arm and think time's gonna fix it. It may heal but it might heal crooked. You gotta attend to it. Realign it. Wrap it up. Then give it time and maybe, just maybe it'll grow back stronger. Me and your daddy suffered a break and /

Avery   You didn't get a chance to wrap it up. Right?

Charles   That's pretty much it.

Baybra *and* **Vince** *enter from the outside.* **Baybra** *is dressed to the nines.*

Baybra   What we got going on in here?

Avery   Hey, Daddy. Hey, Uncle Vince.

Vince   What up, shorty.

Charles   Fellas. (*Beat.*) You looking awfully sharp, baby brother.

Baybra   Yeah, well I didn't have any clothes besides a couple tee shirts I picked up once I got out. Tellulah took me to get some *grown man shit.*

Charles   You say Tellulah got you some new clothes, huh?

Baybra   That's what I said.

Charles   Hmmm . . .

Baybra   What, Charles? You want some praise or something? If it mean that much to you, you can have the damn clothes back.

Charles   Nah I ain't saying all that. I just . . . it was my idea, alright. I just wanted you to know I was thinking about you.

Baybra   . . . Thank you. I'll be sure to pay you back as soon as I get it.

Charles   You ain't gotta do / that.

Baybra   I said I'm gonna pay you back.

Vince   Where's your mama, Avery? What you doing over here?

Avery   Minding my business.

Vince   Oh you so you want to go a few rounds? Big head girl? Dog face!

Avery   Uncle Vince, you big tooth, knocked-kneed, ol' need-a-girlfriend /

Vince   You ol' ashy ankle having, crusty nose, little /

Charles   Alright, alright. Lord. (*Beat.*) So where you been, Baybra, all dressed up?

Baybra   Some bullshit interview. Waste of my damn time.

Charles   On a Saturday?

Vince   I pulled some strings. It went better than he thinks.

Charles   And you're still at the fire station?

Vince   Three days a week, twenty-four hours a day.

Charles   And you can get Baybra in on that? That ain't out his reach?

Baybra   Why you asking him? I'm right here. I can tell you what the man said.

Avery   You gonna be a fireman, Daddy?

Vince   He's gonna be working on the trucks.

Baybra   Y'all motherfuckers gonna keep talking for me or what? Talking 'bout *working on the trucks*, I ain't gonna be working nowhere kissing that white man's ass you introduced me to.

Vince   He's a hard read. I told you that. He wouldn't have talked to you that long if he ain't like you.

Charles   Or . . . you can come on and work with me. It's a sure thing, Baybra. And I keep it Black, you know that about me. Walk in my stores and the only thing white is the milk.

Vince   I think Baybra would rather stand on his own two feet.

Charles   He look like he standing just fine to me.

Vince   Yeah, alright, Charles. (*To* **Avery**.) Hey, Avery, ask your daddy here to take you to play ball sometime. He can play a little bit.

Baybra   A little bit?

Vince   I said what I said. She been learning from me so she might wear your ass out. Look, I gotta get out of here. Let me know if you want to step out tonight.

Baybra   Alright then.

Charles   Now that Baybra's back you oughta start coming by more often, Vince. What you think?

Vince *can't even take this serious; he just half-way smiles and leaves.*

Charles   What's his problem? I say something wrong?

Baybra   Ain't nobody thinking about your funky ass, Charles.

Charles *is at a loss and leaves the kitchen.* **Avery** *just stares at her father. A long awkward moment passes.*

Baybra   Avery . . .

Avery   Daddy . . .

Baybra   Well, what the hell you looking at?

Avery   Mama wanted me to apologize to you when I got the chance. So, I'm sorry for being disrespectful the other night.

Baybra   You don't have to apologize to me.

Avery   Mama says I do, so I do.

Baybra   You always do what you're told?

Avery   When Mama's the one telling me, yes. Things are a lot easier when I do.

Baybra   Well, then, apology accepted. (*Beat.*) So, you're like . . . what, smart as fuck or something? Like how everybody keeps telling me.

Avery   Yeah, I am. You like . . . cuss a lot or something? Like everyone keeps telling me.

Baybra   Yeah I do. But I can do that. Just don't you do it.

Avery   Don't worry. I won't. It sounds stupid to me.

Baybra   Your grandma and your mama go out their way to make sure you ain't nothing like me don't they? Don't do nothing I do. Right? Cause I'm just a loser. Yeah, I see they trying to make you look at me the way my mama used to try and make me look at my daddy. It's okay. I ain't even going to fight it.

Avery   They don't tell me anything. They don't have to. You're like Julio.

Baybra   . . . who the hell is Julio?

Avery   A kid in my class. He does a lot of dumb stuff. Called the teacher out her name. He fights a lot too. He got into a fight one time and fell onto the rabbit cage and killed Mr. Fluffles. He didn't care. He can't even eat lunch with everyone else, they put him in the principal's office to eat. The principal can't even stand him. They come to the cafeteria with us and Julio is in there by himself. Anyways, nobody tells me not to be like you. You're like you. And you got in a lot of trouble for it.

Baybra   . . .

Avery   I'm sorry, Daddy.

Baybra   For what?

Avery   I hurt your feelings. Didn't I?

It's clear she did.

Baybra   What? Hell no.

Avery   Well . . . good. (*Beat.*) I'm going to watch some TV until Mama comes back.

She starts to leave the kitchen but **Baybra** *speaks right before she does.*

Baybra   Say, Avery . . . are you at least glad I'm out?

Avery   I like having someone to call Daddy. Everyone knows my mama and grandma. I never get to tell people *here's my daddy*. I kinda want to show you off. But Grandma said not to get my hopes up. She said most of the time . . . people like you . . .

Baybra   People like me what?

Avery   Aren't around for long.

Baybra   . . .

She leaves. He stays to himself a moment and then **Tellulah** *and* **Vanessa** *enter from the back door.*

Tellulah   So are you going to take it or not? I mean, why not? (*Sees* **Baybra**.) Oh hey, what's up, Baybra? You look good.

Vanessa   You do. Where you going?

Baybra   Nowhere.

Tellulah   Well why you dressed up?

He's still bothered by what **Avery** *said.*

Baybra   Why don't y'all just leave me the hell alone!

He storms out, leaving the house. They aren't offended; in fact they're amused somewhat.

Vanessa   . . . Ol' sensitive ass dude.

Tellulah   Anyways, so you were saying you're about to be moving on up but . . .

Vanessa   But I'm not sure.

Tellulah   Why the hell not? That's a nice raise.

Vanessa   Yeah I know. I just feel like the raise is going to give me an excuse to stay.

Tellulah   And you want to leave?

Vanessa   That was the plan. (*Beat.*) And the plan was for you to come with me.

Tellulah   I mean, if you make a way I'll trudge along.

Vanessa   Why can't you forge a path and I do the trudging, damn it?

Tellulah   Cause I don't have any ideas! You were supposed to get your real estate license, flip houses, make millions, and I was supposed to stage all the houses you sold.

Vanessa   Well . . . let's do that. And you can stop hanging around here all day waiting for Charles to come home.

Tellulah   Excuse me, I don't just *wait* for Charles to come home.

Vanessa   Mmm hmm. Whatchu be doing then?

Tellulah   I . . . man . . . I don't have to tell you shit! I do lots of things. You and Baybra—y'all better stop putting this housewife shit on me.

Vanessa   I ain't say you were a housewife.

Tellulah   You implied it.

Vanessa   You inferred it. I'm just saying we both need to break free. Me from the man and you from *your* man.

Tellulah   I don't want to be free though. In fact, you were just saying how you wish you had a man to smother you. That's what you said. You want him to drape all over you. Said you were ready for that.

Vanessa   Shit and I am ready. Don't mean I can't be thinking of a master plan.

Tellulah   To take over the world?

Vanessa   That's right. And if I meet a brother who wants to be my sidekick then I might allow it.

Tellulah   What about the one dude you were just seeing?

Vanessa   It wasn't going to work. I shouldn't have even entertained him. Should've stuck to my self-imposed restrictions.

Tellulah   What self-imposed restrictions?

Vanessa   I told you already. Remember? If the brother ain't at least forty then he need not apply.

Tellulah   That's right. Your little theory. Let me hear it again.

Vanessa   See, when a man is in his twenties, all he needs is good looks and the slightest potential. Or maybe no potential, if he's that damn fine. He's just a good-looking, broke ass dude and that's okay. But then he hits thirty and his ass may still be fine but if they're broke too, which most of them will be, it stops being okay. So the brothers who actually get a little money, a nice job, good credit, a house—they think they're entitled to some ass because what's your options? The fine, broke brother? Around forty though, men start to learn balance. They slow down. Have confidence but they're not entitled. So then, you just have to pick from the right group of forty-year-olds.

Tellulah   Group?

Vanessa   Well, by forty either they aged well, or they didn't. They're either fit, or they're fucked. Then they're either available or they're not. So obviously you find a fit one who's unattached and at forty I promise you—chances are he's not on the same bullshit the younger guys are. Fifty is right around the corner—they're still young enough to have fun but too old to waste time.

Tellulah   So instead of it being ninety-nine percent likely you're talking to a man who is full of shit, if he's forty plus then . . .?

Vanessa   It goes down to ninety-five percent. The odds are never in your favor, you just go with what gives you the best chance.

Tellulah   Ah hell no. So, let me ask you this then, someone like, let's just say Baybra, is automatically off-limits, correct? Under forty. Sure don't have any money. Can't really check any of your boxes.

Vanessa   Baybra? Why are you bringing up Baybra?

Tellulah   You two seem to have an interesting little energy manifesting.

Vanessa   First off, I believe the energy you're speaking of is called having a kid together. Secondly, yes, he's off-limits because we're in completely different worlds now. There's no reconnecting.

Tellulah   Not even a little? Dinner the other night sure had me fooled.

Vanessa   Baybra and I flirt. We always have. So what? I love Baybra. That ain't gonna change. Besides, Avery was right there, Tellulah. It's good for her to see her parents interacting in a positive way.

Tellulah   Oh that's what it's called nowadays? *Positive interaction?*

Vanessa   That's what *what's* called?

Tellulah   . . .

Vanessa   What?!

Tellulah   You and Baybra boned!

Vanessa   What?! No! Absolutely not.

Tellulah   No?

Vanessa   No!

Tellulah   No?

Vanessa   . . . we may have fooled around just a little. Just a little bit!

Tellulah   I knew it!

Vanessa   It was just a few minutes! And then I realized what I was doing / and—

Tellulah   A few minutes?!

Vanessa   Girl, that's all you need with your brother. The man knows his way around a /

Tellulah   Stop! Fucking yuck! Alright?

Vanessa   Honestly though, I don't even know how it happened. But it won't happen again. I swear.

Tellulah   Girl, I don't care. You two are grown. Been grown. You look good together if you ask me. I mean, he may be a little mentally and emotionally stunted for you. Maybe you can help that. I don't know. But I knew something was there. Always has been. Long before Avery. I knew he still had you on the brain, I just didn't know if it was mutual.

Vanessa   It's not. I saw a good-looking man who was looking at me like ain't a damn thing ever been made better and since I was due for a little pick-me-up, I indulged him. He also happens to be the father of my child so who cares? We did it. It was good. We've moved on.

Tellulah   And Baybra's on the same page?

Vanessa   Ain't but one page to be on. I'm writing this story and there's only one page. One chapter. One part. One point. And the title of it all is *Avery*. It ain't about us no more. He can be on that page or he can pick up another damn book. (*Beat.*) Plus, look how Baybra's acting. All that shit between you, him, and Charles. I don't see myself wanting to be mixed up in all of that.

Tellulah   Please. I could go the rest of my life without talking about that.

Vanessa   What are you going to do about them? How you going to fix it?

Tellulah   Ain't for me to fix. Baybra doesn't like Charles. He's made that known. Okay, fine. Whatever. But me and him ain't about to negotiate how I live my life.

Vanessa   I get that. But maybe / he—

Tellulah   And I'll tell you what else, he's selfish. Just like my daddy. He picks and chooses what he wants to forget and what he wants to remember. It's always so goddamn convenient.

Vanessa   Maybe he has a legitimate reason why he can't simply forget.

Tellulah   Legitimate? Let me tell you what Baybra can't let go of—it ain't what Charles did but it's the fact he had the audacity to do it as if Baybra wouldn't do shit about it. It ain't been about me for a long time.

Vanessa   Just to play devil's advocate, what if it is about you? Maybe he's genuinely worried about you.

Tellulah   Worried about me how?

Vanessa   Worried that Charles is . . . you know . . . not acting right.

Tellulah   Not acting right how?

Vanessa   Still putting his hands on you.

Tellulah   That's what Baybra said?

Vanessa   That's what he told me.

Tellulah   Of course he's going to think that. Baybra hasn't changed one bit. So he doesn't want to acknowledge that someone else could have. Baybra's in some time warp. He thinks he got locked up and the world stopped and waited for him.

Vanessa   . . . okay.

Tellulah   Okay?

Vanessa   Yeah. Okay.

Tellulah   What's on your mind, Vanessa? Why you holding back? Just say whatever you gotta say.

Vanessa   I used to ask you something just as a courtesy. But I already knew the answer. I could look at you and look through you and know everything I wanted to know. Now, I just have to ask and believe you. Not that you'd lie but . . . I don't know . . . we're not having the conversations no one can hear anymore. Not like we used to. People used to walk in on us and we'd get quiet. Seems like you and Charles do that nowadays. And that's your husband. God knows you got the right to do it. It just wouldn't be a complete surprise if things were going on that I couldn't get a straight answer about.

Tellulah   Then just ask, I'll give it to you straight.

Vanessa   Is Charles putting his hands on you?

Tellulah   No.

Vanessa   Okay.

Tellulah   Listen, we're still working through things. That's marriage. It's been a long road. Not because of any one thing. There's always going to be something. But maybe, I just don't want to bore you with all the details. Sure, sometimes things are strange still / but me and Charles—

This triggers **Vanessa**.

Vanessa   Strange how?!

Tellulah   Vanessa, shit is strange sometimes when you wake up every day next to the same person.

Vanessa   And that's all it is? Nothing more.

Tellulah   Nothing more.

Vanessa   Okay. But you might want to talk to Baybra though. You know how he can be.

Tellulah   I'll talk to him.

Vanessa   And you might want to talk to your mother. As I understand it, she's the source. She's the one who told your daddy who then told Baybra, told him things like you being pregnant but losing the baby . . . because of Charles.

Tellulah   . . .

Vanessa   Tellulah?

Tellulah   . . . yeah, I don't know. I'll talk to Baybra. I'll straighten it out.

Scene Four

Baybra *sits at the table talking with* **Vince**. **Baybra** *is drinking straight from a small bottle of whiskey and* **Vince** *has a small glass, presumably one* **Baybra** *keeps refilling for him. They're not drunk . . . just feeling pretty good.*

Baybra   All because of a tattoo?

Vince   Yeah man, it hit me. You know?

Baybra   Nah. I don't. Tell me again—*when the half-gods* . . . what? How it go?

Vince   *Heartily know, when the half-gods go, the Gods arrive.*

Baybra (*laughs*)   I guess whatever speaks to you, my man.

Vince   You ain't thinking enough about it. I'm laying up with that woman every night, thinking she can't do no better than me. As soon as I leave she get that tattoo and all that means is *thank you, nigga, thank you for leaving. Now the real man, a real God can come to me. Because you was just a half-god.* Or maybe now, she intends on becoming the God herself. Either way, I was in her way. That shit is heavy. Hell, not even just about love, how many times are we just standing in the way of something bigger and better. I don't know, that shit fucks me up.

Baybra   You would've thought you were the one in jail. I get out and you here reciting poetry and quotes from dead white men. Philosophizing and shit.

Vince   Just giving you some inspiration, brother. Don't allow yourself to be the type of motherfucker people will be better without. I know I'm not.

He finishes his drink and stands up and starts to leave.

I gotta work tomorrow, let me get out of here.

Baybra   Alright then.

Charles *enters.*

Charles   Fellas.

Vince   What's going on, man?

Charles   Nothing much. You ain't gotta leave on account of me.

Vince   I was heading out anyways. I'll get at you, Baybra.

He leaves.

Charles   Where's your sister, baby brother?

Baybra   Out with Vanessa.

Charles   I thought you and Vince would've been out too. Friday night. You gotta enjoy it.

Baybra   Nah, ain't nothing for me to get into really.

Charles *makes an innuendo. Even shoves* **Baybra** *with his elbow and laughs.*

Charles   Nothing to get into, or *nobody to get into*?

Baybra   Good one, Charles. Let me ask you something, why is that your new thing, man? Trying to talk to me like we're boys or something?

Charles   I'm just talking to you like we're men.

Baybra   Oh okay. So this is man-talk? Just a couple fellas in the locker room talking about bitches and shit.

Charles   Well, I wasn't going to put it that way.

Baybra   But that's what you were implying right?

Imitates him.

You ain't got nothing to get into or NOBODY *to get into, baby brother . . . ha-ha-ha-ha.*

Charles   Alright, Baybra, never mind. Your sister was giving me hell earlier today. I'm not looking for trouble with you. I should've kept it moving.

Baybra   Nah, it's cool. Let's talk like men. You know, I guess I do got a little someone I could call up. I met this chick a couple nights ago while I was out with Vince. Big ass titties, man. You should've seen 'em. And they'll surprise you. Because her body is pretty modest when she's fully clothed. Well, she can't hide that ass. It jumps out at you from hello. And even without all that body her face is the prettiest thing I ever saw. It's the darkest part on her too. You wouldn't know it unless you stared at her. And I stared. I studied her tall ass. A Nubian goddess. Skin black as coffee with gorgeous locs. Anyways, I go back to her place, we drink, talk a little bit, and next thing I know I got her long ass legs spread across all seven continents. I went to town. I laid the pipe! You feel me? Fucked her . . . real good. All night long. Truth be told I can't stop thinking about her. (*Beat.*) Is that the man-talk you looking for? You like that don't you? Look at you. Sweating. An old nigga like you ain't got the drive for that no more do you?

Charles   I ain't that damn old.

Baybra   You just an old horny nigga trying to live vicariously through some young blood. Say no more, next time I go to her house I'll make sure when I pull them panties off I stuff them in my pocket. Then you can have them. Sniff 'em all you want. Don't worry. I won't tell Tellulah. Cause we just having man-talk. Right?

Charles   Alright, Baybra, whatever.

He is about to leave the kitchen but **Baybra** *stops him at the last second.*

Baybra   Come on, sit down. I'm joking with you. Shit. I forgot I'm talking to an ol' polishes up deacon.

He pours a glass of orange juice for **Charles**.

Baybra   There, have a drink with me.

Charles   Boy, you crazy, you know that?

Baybra   I know. Hey, look who I was brought up around. My old man. (*Beat.*) You.

Charles   Well, I don't /

Baybra   Come on now, Charles. For all the talking you do about my pops back in the day, you act like I didn't get a good look at you too. *Chuckie Ray! All damn day!*

Charles   Ah hell, I ain't heard that in so long.

Baybra   You and my pops were some wild cats.

Charles   You right. I was . . . something else.

Bayra   Something else? Come on, Chuckie Ray! Say what you really mean?

Charles   I was a real motherfucker, alright?!

Baybra   There he is!

Charles   Man, give me a taste of that whiskey!

Baybra *gives him his bottle he's still sipping from.*

Baybra   Ah shit! Look at him! Tellulah ain't gonna give you no whooping is she?

Charles   What she doesn't know won't hurt her.

Baybra   I say the same thing with regards to my P.O.

Charles   No, no, no. I ain't going that far, Baybra. You gotta do the right thing. You hear me?

Baybra   Yeah, I hear you. Just don't have much motivation. Freedom is overrated. What Dr. King say? Being free to do a lot of shit that your pockets won't let you do is freedom and famine at the same fucking time.

Charles   I think you're paraphrasing. But I get the gist. That's why I told you to come work with me. I'll pay you good. Some days are long but I'll pay you good.

Baybra   I just want something for myself. You know?

Charles   You got something. You got a chance to start over.

Baybra   Please. Most people I run into, they know I did some time and their eyes say it all. What's this nigga doing out here on these streets amongst us good civilians? Especially the white folks who handing out the jobs. See, you gotta have a gimmick to be worth anything to these people. Gotta be a magical negro. A virtuoso. I gotta have an uncanny penchant for math. Or a secret talent. The violin or some shit.

Something they can look and say where that nigga learn to do something niggas ain't supposed to do. If they can show a nigga off at Carnegie Hall and say they discovered me, they saved me, they resurrected me, if my life serves them then I'm worth a second shot. Otherwise, I'm just a regular ol' nigga who better make something happen off this seven twenty-five an hour. And all I'm saying is it might be worth risking this limited ass freedom to live a life worth living until I'm caught. (*Beat.*) My own daughter looking at me like I'm nothing. Took her ten years to form the opinion she has of me now, I ain't got the time to change it. My own daughter, man. Only ever been one person to look at me like I meant something.

Charles   Tellulah.

Baybra   Damn right. She's all I ever had to be honest. That's my girl, man. Love her. You know? There's things she knows about me no one else would ever know. She's saved my life so many times in so many ways.

Charles   I've been there too, Baybra. At the edge of hell begging the devil to let me in. I've imagined making myself null and damn void in every way possible. Thought of ways to torture myself. I ain't talking no one time and I ain't talking no long time ago. But your sister convinced me that wasn't meant for me. There's a lot of shit I've done that I can't come back from and your sister was my only salvation. If she told me there was no coming back with her, if she ever said it . . . I don't think I could make it.

Baybra   Sometimes I be in my own head and I'd see her there. In my head. I'm thinking how the hell you get in here? She's always been there for me and I can't say I've been there to save her once.

Charles   Some people are simply meant to be the ones doing the saving.

Baybra   Yeah, I guess. (*Beat.*) My precious Tulips. I bet you ain't ever heard nobody call her that.

Charles   Can't say that I have.

Baybra   My folks use to call her Tellu-lips. Daddy said Tellulah's name sounded like an old lady's name so he just made up Tellu-lips. Sounded like the flower I guess. But see, that shit was ugly too so I just took it all the way there. Tulips. My precious Tulips. She hated when I said that though. After a while, when Daddy wasn't around and Mama just started calling her by her name again. I kept calling her Tulips. I'm the only one who could get away with it. I call her that when I need to talk to her about something. Nobody knows that. Not even Vanessa. I always wondered if you did.

Charles   Nah, never knew.

Baybra   It's little things like that I hold onto to remind myself who I am to her. Because lately I can't tell. She acts like we're nothing special.

Charles   That's not true. Your sister is crazy about you.

Baybra   Nah. She loves me. But it ain't the same. She don't even think I got the right to worry about her. Her life is hers and mine is mine. And the two don't intersect no more.

Charles   You don't have to worry about her, Baybra.

Baybra   Yeah, well, not to ruin a good thing here but you can see why coming from you, that don't mean shit.

Charles   Yeah, I get it.

Baybra   So, because I am worried about her and because she won't let me in, I'm going to bring it to you. In the spirit of us having *man-talk*.

Charles   Alright.

Baybra   You still putting your hands on my sister?

Charles   No.

Baybra   Never?

Charles   Not ever. I'm telling you what God loves.

Baybra   Don't do that, Charles. Don't sit here and drink my whiskey, bullshit with me, and share the first good moment we done had in a while and end it on a bad note by lying to me.

Charles   I'm not lying to you.

Baybra   I'm not saying recently. I'm saying ever. Did you ever put your hands on her again? You can tell me. This is how we start over. With the truth.

Charles   And I'm saying no, not ever. It was that one time, Baybra. That's it.

Baybra *erupts.*

Baybra   I said don't lie to me, motherfucker!

Charles *matches* **Baybra**'s *rage.*

Charles   I'm not going to keep going through this with you, little nigga! Now, I've done all the ass kissing I can do. But it ain't going any further than this.

Baybra   It'll go however far I say it'll go! I'll drag your Black ass to hell if I got to, nigga!

Charles   You think I want this? We can argue. We can disagree. I can be every motherfucker in the book. But you my wife's brother. But I ain't gonna fight you, Baybra.

Baybra   You ain't shit but a bitch. Just like I thought.

Charles   Why you doing this, man?

Baybra   Tell me the truth.

Charles   I told you but I ain't what you want to hear.

Baybra   I'm not gonna keep begging you for it, Charles.

Charles   Alright, you want the truth? Me and your sister ain't been right in a long time. Even before I did what I did. Damn sure not afterwards.

Baybra   I'm so damn tired of everyone calling it that. When Charles did what he did. Ain't nothing wrong in calling a dead horse dead, nigga. Call it what it was. What did you do? Own up to it!

Charles   Before I jumped on her and beat her down! Alright?! And when she wouldn't stop talking I started to punch her! Hard! Like she was a man! Until finally she wasn't talking. She wasn't making no sound. And my knuckles were raw and bruised. Until I almost killed her! That's what I did. And not a single day has gone by where I haven't thought about just disappearing and killing my damn self. That's what I was telling you. I still carry it! And I hate it! But God, boy . . . God has shown me grace and I ain't gonna refuse it.

Baybra   That's how you sleep at night? Convinced yourself to just let go? And let God? You shouldn't have to carry anything with you because everything can be forgiven. It's that simple?

Charles (*damn near sermon like*)   Nah it's anything but simple. But salvation is real. Forgiveness: it exists, baby brother. But ain't nobody said nothing about it being pretty. It ain't just saying everything is okay. Or erasing something from your memory. It's telling someone you gonna do better and them giving you a chance to prove it; but it don't all come at once. Me and your sister been going through hell. Sometimes things are fine. Then there's mornings she wakes up and looks at me like it's ten years ago. And she's talking through her teeth to keep herself from calling me every name in the book. She hasn't let me touch her but maybe five times. In eight, nine years, man. Sure, we've hugged. But I'm talking about touching her how a man is supposed to touch his wife. I'm telling you, man, it's hard to look at a woman like she's your wife when you know the sight of you disgusts her. Forgiveness isn't pretty, Baybra. It's a journey. It's an agreement. It's saying I'm going to do better and someone saying I'll give you the chance to prove it. But it don't come all at once.

He gets on his knees.

See, I got down. Everyday. I crawled, following your sister around.

Baybra   Get off your damn knees man.

Charles   No, I want you to see it. I crawled after her. Every day for a month straight. I wasn't worthy to walk behind her. I crawled until my knees bled and scabbed over. Begging for her forgiveness, with my hands clasped so tight my fingers swelled up. I couldn't even straighten them out. And when she said she forgave me the first time, I kept crawling. Every day until she finally said it and I knew she at least meant just a little of it. Somedays it feels like I'm still crawling and that's alright. Because I'll fight for her forgiveness. I'll fight for yours too, brother, if you'd let me. I. Am. Sorry. Baby Brother.

He is standing again and **Baybra** *becomes enraged.*

Baybra   I don't want the performance, Charles! I don't want the scriptures or the sermons! I want the truth. And then you can have my forgiveness. I wanna know why it's taken her ten years to forgive your sorry ass, huh? Maybe because it hasn't been no ten years. You get mad sometimes and you hit her don't you? She was pregnant and you still hit her. Didn't you?

Charles   What? No! / Hell no!

Baybra *pulls out a gun and rushes* **Charles**, *pushing him against the wall, putting the gun to his head.*

Baybra   Shut your ass up! And tell me the truth! Don't open your mouth to say nothing but the truth! I swear to God, Charles, I ain't playing with you no more.

Charles (*begging, pleading, scared*)   Alright! Alright, Baybra . . . I'll tell you!

Act Two

Scene One

Lights are dim on **Vanessa** *and* **Vince**. *They sit at the kitchen table, statuesque. They are looking in the direction of but do not react to* **Charles** *and* **Tellulah** *who are near the island and fully lit.*

Tellulah   What are you doing, Charles? Huh? What are you doing?

Charles   Baybra is filled with rage. Alright? He's going to keep throwing punches. Now, if I become a wall and stand rigid and firm while he's throwing these punches, something bad is bound to happen. I'm going to eventually crack and he's likely to hurt himself too.

Tellulah   Oh God! More metaphors and parables.

Charles   Jesus spoke in parables.

Tellulah   Yeah and you ain't Him.

Charles   I'm softening myself. I'll absorb his blows. I ain't got nothing in me but love for Baybra. So when he throws those punches he ain't gonna hurt me and he ain't gonna hurt himself. He'll tire out if anything and then he'll see only love and communication and understanding is going to solve this.

Tellulah   Baybra doesn't love you, Charles. He doesn't want to communicate with you and he doesn't want to understand you. I told you what to expect and you thought you knew better. His mind is made up. He's sick with this shit. Like my father. Can't let a damn thing go. It's a disease and he don't know it. And you think you got the cure but we talked about this.

Charles   You talked. I listened.

Tellulah   Don't do that. (*Beat.*) Don't do that.

Charles   I'm not going toe to toe with him. I won't do it.

Tellulah   I don't want this in our house. It ain't built for this. We start reliving things, things we've agreed to move beyond, and the walls are going to come down.

Charles   Maybe this is the reality check we need, baby. Maybe we need somebody to challenge us. Are we who we say we are? Are we better than what we were?

Tellulah   Well, you ain't beating the shit out of me right now so I'd say yeah.

Charles   And that's just it, we ain't standing in the mud no more but we never washed it off. So we're just walking around with it stuck to us. We ain't really moved on.

Tellulah   Well, it's not because I'm hanging it over your head.

Charles   But it's hanging there nonetheless somehow. You don't see that? Baybra been here two weeks and he sees it. He tries to get between you and me and he does it with ease. How is that? I'll tell you how, there's space between us, baby. He's got room to slide right in there. We've been exposed. We need to close this gap between us once and for all.

Tellulah   We need Baybra to get the hell out of our house.

Charles   He's your brother. You want him gone? You put him out?

Tellulah   No, *you* do it, Charles! This is your house. I am your wife. Be a man! You know what that is? You need me to give you an example? Huh? BE A MAN!

Charles *erupts. He slams his fists; he throws whatever is nearest.* **Tellulah** *flinches but doesn't retreat.*

Charles   I AM GODDAMMIT! You looking at a man if you ain't looking at nothing else! (*Beat.*) I am a man. Don't . . . don't . . . you don't need to do that. Don't do that, Tellulah.

Tellulah   We get along for the most part. Don't we? No, it's not perfect but we get along. We have a flow. It works for us. Now, Baybra comes here and we've been arguing for two weeks straight.

Charles   Cause we been walking around like we're dead. Without feelings. Like robots. And we got our routine down, don't we? But Baybra woke us up. (*Beat.*) You know . . . every time Vanessa comes around my dick gets hard.

Tellulah   Excuse me?

Charles   Yeah. Because you're you again when she's here. For her, you gonna be that same ol' Tellulah. You're sexy and funny and you flirt with me and I can't take my eyes off you.

Tellulah   I'm all of those things when it's just you and me, too.

Charles   No. You show glimpses but Vanessa's the catalyst. And I get it. If you can prove to her everything is fine, then everyone else will believe it too.

Tellulah   Fine. You're the victim. I'm mistreating you so badly. I'm so sorry, Charles, that you're living in hell.

Charles   Nah, I ain't saying that. But I am saying that it ain't no secret what's between us. Our little flow ain't working no more. We can't fake it no more. (*Beat.*) Everyone wanted to know how you could stay with me; why'd you stay. And now I'm asking too. Why did you? Why'd you stay, Tellulah?

Tellulah   Sometimes I wonder that my damn self.

He's stunned for a moment. **Tellulah** *makes her way to the table with* **Vince** *and* **Vanessa**. *The light shifts and the kitchen is fully lit.* **Charles** *disappears.*

Tellulah   That was the last conversation we had. He left after that, to clear his head I guess. Baybra seen him later that night but at some point he left again. And that was that.

Vanessa   Why you just now telling us this?

Tellulah   I thought he'd be back by now. I don't know. Thought he was just clearing his head.

Vanessa   Maybe he is. Three days isn't that long. I mean . . . it is but maybe he just needs some space. Look, tell me what we can do. Give us something. Some way to help.

Tellulah   There's nothing really.

Vince   What about the stores? Want me to go check on things?

Tellulah   Baybra's been helping. Or trying to at least. If they're not open when they're supposed to be Charles is going to come back to a dead ass business. He knows that.

Vanessa   Good thing you got Baybra.

Tellulah   Yeah, good thing. (*Beat.*) He's got something to do with this.

Vince   Who? Baybra? How he got something to do with it?

Tellulah   He did something. He said something. He knows something. That's how.

Vanessa   I don't think Baybra would go that far, Tellulah.

Tellulah   How you know how far he'll go? The most you know about him, I told you. He ain't ever let you in. Fucking on a kitchen counter don't make you soulmates. I don't care if you gotta kid by him or not. I know him! So don't sit here telling me what he would or wouldn't do.

Vanessa   You're emotional and / you're not—

Tellulah   I know what I'm / talking about.

Vanessa   No! Listen to me. You're not talking to someone who's indebted to you. I'm not Baybra and I'm not Charles. So you don't get to say whatever the fuck you want to me. You're my sister. And my friend. And I love you. But don't get besides yourself, Tellulah. Not with me.

Her phone rings. She grabs it.

I gotta take this. (*On phone.*) Hello? (*Beat.*) Hey, sure I can talk. (*Beat.*) I left them there at my desk. They're there.

She leaves the kitchen.

Vince   That was a little harsh.

Tellulah   . . .

Vince   You know what I think? I think this is a huge adjustment for everybody involved. You. Vanessa. Avery. Charles. Not me. Baybra ain't ever been no burden for me. Hell, him being home ain't nothing but good news for me. I got my main man back. But for you all? I can see how it could be a lot. And Charles is used to being the head nigga in charge around here. The alpha dog. Baybra is infringing on that and maybe he just needed to step away. Probably drunk a little too much. Spent a little too much money and waiting for things to cool down.

Tellulah   I've never known you to be so optimistic, Vince.

Vince   Well, I'm not. I'm being realistic. And I think what I just said is the most realistic scenario.

Tellulah   And *realistically* Baybra ain't got nothing to do with it?

Vince   . . .

Tellulah   How did you and Vanessa turn out so good and me and Baybra so fucked-up?

Vince   Come on now, don't do that. That ain't you. I ain't gonna let you pity yourself.

Tellulah   I'm just saying, you and her get together and talk about good things. Civil things. Me and Baybra talk about nothing good. Ever. No good in either of our lives.

Vince   Tellulah, baby, I know shit is / crazy right now but—

Tellulah   No, I'm not asking you to tell me it's better than what they seem. I'm a housewife in a house given to my husband. I didn't even pick the damn curtains. I have no career. My husband runs a few corner stores. Again, given to him. Family house, family business, family money. A lot of money but it ain't really mine. And now *this*. Look at you then look at me. We were next-door neighbors for God's sake. Went to the same school.

Vince   I ain't gonna tell you that you and Baybra ain't been through some shit. We both know you have. And I ain't gonna act clueless either, sis. Your folks did a number on y'all. But, our parents weren't no saints either. I think we all turned out okay. Everyone's folks make mistakes.

Tellulah   And what did your parents do? You ever saw them fight? With their fists? Did they blame you two for their problems? Did your intelligence insult them? Because at twelve you figured out that they would be better off without each other. Did they curse you out for not crying anymore when they would throw things and assault each other in the middle of the night? *HOW DARE YOU IMPLY IT'S NORMAL, TELLULAH! YOU'RE TOO GROWN TO CRY?* Or did your parents just argue about what cereal to buy? The sugary kind or something with a little more fiber? Because I was there for that argument . . . if that's what you want to call it.

Vince   So you had the worst life imaginable. No wonder why Baybra went to prison. No wonder why you married Charles and sit around here hating every second of your life. God only knows how you all ain't in a padded room chewing on your hair.

Tellulah   Fuck you, Vince.

Vince   Hey! I'm not gonna pity you. The average motherfucker would've crumbled a long time ago. You didn't. So I don't expect you to now. You set the bar high. Now, let's be objective about the shit, what you need me to do?

Tellulah   Talk to Baybra.

Vince   I do talk to him. When all of you turned your backs on him and stopped visiting and writing I was the nigga up there once a month.

Tellulah   Talk to him about Charles.

Vince   Why?

Tellulah   What do you mean why? My husband is missing, Vince.

Vince   Tellulah, listen, alright? You don't understand exactly who Baybra is anymore.

Tellulah   And you do?

Vince   Nah, that's the thing, nobody does. At least I understand that. You all keep getting disappointed, but I don't, because I realized before he even got locked up that I don't know that nigga. I know what he was. Who he was to me. And I'll love him forever cause of it. But all we know now is he sat up there for ten years thinking about shit. We all know that. *You* know that. And you still welcomed him here, in your home, with open arms.

Tellulah   You saying I wanted this?

Vince   I'm saying let's keep praying for Charles and whatever comes from that, let it come. Cause either you're right about Baybra or wrong about Charles.

Vanessa *comes back in, but they don't see her. She listens.*

Tellulah   Wrong how?

Vince   Maybe the nigga just left you. Let it stay up in the air, sis.

Tellulah   Again . . . fuck you, Vince. I want to know.

Vanessa (*abruptly*)   Alright. I'll talk to him.

Tellulah   You can't just come out and ask him . . .

Vanessa   I know how to talk to him.

Tellulah *turns her attention to* **Vince***. He delays.*

Vince   And what if there's something to know? I don't think there is, but what if? You gonna turn him in? Huh? What about you, Vanessa? It's Baybra; that's who we talking about.

Tellulah   I know who the hell he is!

Vince   . . . alright. I'll see what he'll tell me. I don't think he's got anything to tell, but I'll see.

Vanessa   And when we come back telling you that you're wrong, that's the end of it.

Tellulah   *If* I'm wrong. Yeah, that's the end of it.

Scene Two

Lights up on **Vanessa** *and* **Baybra**.

Vanessa   So how's everything? Business good?

Baybra   I guess. I'm just trying to keep up.

Vanessa   I'm sure whatever you're doing is better than nothing at all.

Baybra   Ain't really my thing, you know? But I figure it's the least I can do for Tellulah. Charles too.

Vanessa   Are you scared? You know, for Charles?

Baybra   Nah. I ain't gonna sit here and lie, talking about I'm scared. But I didn't want anything to happen to the man.

Vanessa   But you do think something happened?

Baybra   I don't know.

Vanessa   I'm just asking, what do you think?

A moment.

Baybra   Well, I think he was still putting his hands on my sister. I think the guilt was getting to him. I think he knew it was only a matter of time before I could prove it and you and everyone else found out. It was only a matter of time until he did it again. Put that with the fact I believe he was still drinking . . . heavily.

Vanessa   I haven't even seen him in the same room as an open bottle, Baybra.

Baybra   I saw him drinking. I was sipping on a little something and he asked me for it. Snatched it right out of my hand.

Vanessa   And why would he be that comfortable around you?

Baybra   Probably so I'd be comfortable around him.

Vanessa   . . . I don't know, Baybra.

Baybra   Well, I know. I know the guilt, the paranoia, him knowing I wasn't going to just drop it, him drinking again, had his mind in a million different places. Charles is weak, you understand? It was too much for him. And somehow, somewhere out there, he got himself in some trouble. Got robbed, got jumped, hell, fell in a ditch. I don't know. Whatever it was, there wasn't no coming back from.

Vanessa   You think . . . Charles is . . . gone *gone*? Like for good?

Baybra   It's been a couple weeks now, Vanessa. You were here when all his people were, his employees, everyone else. Nobody's seen him. Nobody's heard from him. What's left to think? You think someone kidnapped his ass? Holding him for ransom?

Vanessa   Maybe.

Baybra   The man don't make that much damn money. I think everybody needs to accept it and just move on already. Especially Tellulah.

Vanessa   Move on? You're definitely eager, aren't you?

Baybra   That's what folks been telling me to do. Say it'll solve all of life's problems. Move on and act like shit ain't ever happened.

Vanessa   I never said that.

Baybra   Everything don't have to be said all the time.

She takes her time.

Vanessa   I wish I would've just listened to you.

Baybra   Yeah? About what?

Vanessa   I should've been more aware of what's been going on around here.

Baybra   So then . . . you know . . . you think he was? Up to that same ol' shit?

Vanessa   I don't know. Maybe. Not sure how I missed it though.

Baybra   Don't do that. Don't blame yourself for none of this. You've been right up under them. Can't see the forest for the trees.

Vanessa   Well, I know this much, if he was hitting her, I mean even a shove or if he breathed too heavy in her direction then he's fallen out of grace with me. (*Beat.*) Baybra . . .

Baybra   What's up?

Vanessa   You can tell me, you know.

Baybra   Tell you what?

Vanessa   If you know anything.

Baybra   Know anything?

Vanessa   . . .

Baybra   About Charles?

Vanessa   I mean . . . yeah. Anything at all. Whatever it is.

Baybra   I doubt I could, Vanessa. And I don't say that to implicate myself because, like I said, I don't know anything except you want to take some information back to my sister. But I got nothing.

Vanessa   No, that's not it. It ain't about Tellulah. I'd want to know for myself. And if you asked me to keep it between us I would.

Baybra   You would, would you?

Vanessa   Baybra look, I was wrong. With or without Tellulah, we're Vanessa and Baybra. Even without Avery. Add her in though and it definitely means a whole lot more. But I can be there for you. I should've said this to you a long time ago. I thought I showed it. But I could've said it.

Baybra   Shouldas, couldas, wouldas, right?

Vanessa   I'm serious, Baybra. I know more than you think. What you've been through. I should've been there. I'm trying to be here now. You don't have to carry everything on your own.

Baybra   Where is all this coming from?

Vanessa   Everything is so fucking fragile right now. Charles is gone. Tellulah is scared. I'm trying to help but there's nothing I can do. I guess I'm just in my head. Thinking. And so naturally I'm thinking about you. Wishing I would've done things differently. Because I don't want to be useless. I want to be there for you as much as I want to be there for her. Maybe more. You don't have to pretend things never happened. Nothing that may be going on now and nothing that happened while you were growing up. I'm here for you.

Baybra   Vanessa, listen, I'm cool. Alright? I'm fine. Always have been.

Vanessa   But you're not. You've *been* hurting, Baybra. And we all failed you. Made you feel like you had to hold it all inside because we all hold something; but it doesn't stack up to what you gotta bear. And I'm saying you can let it all go. Right here. Beginning to end. (*Beat.*) I know about your mother. I know your father stepped out on her and had you by another woman and that woman left soon as you were born. I know once your father left, you wanted to go with him but he wouldn't take you so you just stayed with your mother and Tellulah. That's why you felt like she favored Tellulah. Even pushed you off on her so she wouldn't have to deal with you as much.

Baybra   Okay, so you know. Now I'm supposed to pour my heart out to you? Tell you how it scarred me? Ruined me? How I want to be someone else? Something else?

Vanessa   Do you?

Baybra   I want to be the same motherfucker who beat that kid's head in for stealing my money!

Vanessa   Okay, so now that you're clearly still him, what now?

Baybra   Don't patronize me, Vanessa.

Vanessa   I'm not.

Baybra   Don't try and handle me goddammit!

Vanessa   . . . I'm just trying to be there for you.

Baybra   Be there? Where? I see your ass. You right here. Appreciate it. Thank you. God bless you for it. All that shit. Now, you can't stop talking to me about this shit. When I wanted to talk you're right, all of you told me to kiss your ass. You ain't want to hear it. So that's that. Now we talking about Charles. The nigga is gone. My real mama, my fake mama, my daddy's ass ain't got nothing to do with it.

Vanessa *sidesteps his building anger and frustration. She continues, cautiously.*

Vanessa   Tellulah used to feel so guilty for understanding why your mother treated you the way she did. It wasn't right but she understood it. And she couldn't change it. So she loved you enough for both of them. I'm not saying your mother didn't love you / I'm just—

Baybra   I am. But at least she was decent enough to not just throw me away. She fed me. She clothed me. I remember a few kisses here and there when I was younger. Things were different the older I got though. Tellulah's attitude was hey can you blame her? It's Daddy's fault. And my attitude was fuck yeah I can. But I never expected nor wanted Tellulah to give up Mama. Not for me. She proved herself in other ways. (*Beat.*) Mama dated this one cat before Tony. Dude was always in my face about something. Mama figured I needed a male presence. Daddy was dropping off money but he wasn't coming around like he should've been. So one night, this cat got on me after some basketball game. I wasn't playing hard enough, I guess. On the way home he tells me I'm going to run around the block a hundred times before I go to bed. Mama was pulling a graveyard shift, she wasn't there. So, we get home and dude keeps trying to make me run. But I wouldn't move. I said, man call my mama and tell her what you're doing. He said when it's just me and him I ain't got no mama. I ain't got nothing. I said, well I got God. He said I'm God, little nigga! And I'll tell you the truth, I think the motherfucker believed that. Then he took his belt off and wrapped it around my neck and starts running full speed. I keep up for a few seconds but the nigga was fast. I'll give him that. So, I fall and he drags me for like ten feet. My knees are scraped up. I busted my lip. Cosmetic shit really, but still. Tellulah then calls Mama to tell her. My mama was bothered, she was upset, but there wasn't any real urgency. She said she'll handle it when she gets off. Well, Tellulah didn't want to wait that long. She finds this dude sleeping on the couch with a cigarette in his mouth. All of a sudden, I hear *pssssss* . . . *Baybra, come here!* So, I go downstairs and she's holding this lit cigarette. She blows on the end of it to make it burn a little hotter. Then she sticks it right in his motherfucking eye! He jumps up screaming like a little bitch. Whistling damn near. And Tellulah said *well you got a flame in your eye, nigga, but you don't sound like the roar of a many waters so you must not be God after all.* Yeah, she did that shit. Tellulah don't owe me nothing. Neither do you. You gave me Avery. Vince gave me loyalty. I'm good.

Vanessa   But Tellulah isn't. So, give her peace of mind.

Baybra   I can't give her that. If I could, I would. She gonna have to find it like I did.

Vanessa   But did you?

Baybra   . . .

Vanessa   Look at me, we ain't ever lied to each other. If you know something just tell me. I'll find a way to give it to Tellulah so she doesn't know any more than she needs to. But she needs to know something.

Baybra   I got nothing.

Someone knocks at the back door.

That's Vince. (*Towards door.*) Come on!

Vince *enters.*

Vince   Good people, what's happening?

Baybra   You got it.

Vanessa   Hey, I actually was just about to leave to go pick up Avery from school.

Vince   Where's Tellulah?

Baybra   Her and my mama went to talk to some of Charles' family. They're trying to take over the stores or some shit. Tellulah's trying to be fair about it but . . . we'll see.

Vince   That don't seem right.

Baybra   That's how them people do.

Vanessa   Well, I'll talk to you all later.

Vince   Alright then.

Vanessa *leaves.*

Vince   You still been working at the stores or his family took that over too?

Baybra   Nah, I've been up there.

Vince   You gonna need some help? I know a few folks looking for some work.

Baybra   Nah, things been pretty slow. I don't know what kinda people-person Charles was but them same folks don't come and see me.

Vince   Smile more. I've always told you that. You gotta nice smile. Ain't as nice as mine, but I'm sure a few folks like it.

Baybra   Shit, your sister love it.

Vince   Don't do that, nigga.

A forced segue.

So any word on Charles?

Baybra   Nothing that I know of.

Vince   I hate to hear it and God forbid anything happened to him, but he always rubbed me the wrong way if I'm being honest.

Baybra   What you talking about?

Vince   He was always all over the place. Fickle. He was either trying to act older than he was or act younger. Wanted people to think he was this straight-laced deacon but I heard stories of how he talked to some of them younger cats who worked for him. He was going to do whatever he could get away with. Truth be told, I never got over what he did to Tellulah.

Baybra   . . .

Vince   Let me cut the bullshit, between you and me, Baybra . . . we can talk, right? You and me?

Baybra   We the only ones here. Us and these walls.

Vince   My man. (*Beat.*) So between you and me, I don't blame you.

Baybra   Blame me for what?

Vince   Doing what you did.

Baybra   What the fuck I do?

Vince   You know . . . Charles. I know you took care of that shit. I saw it in your eyes when I picked you up. I knew you wasn't going to let him slide. Not ten years later, not a hundred years later.

Baybra   Nah, you got it all wrong, Vince.

Vince   Do I?

Baybra   Man I swear, between you and your sister, I'm on trial all over again. Listen, all I ever did / was just talk to the man.

Vince   Whoa, whoa, whoa. Hold on, Baybra. Don't tell me nothing. Plausible deniability. The less I know, the better I am. Needless to say if shit starts to cave in on you, I gotta cat who will represent you . . . pro bono of course. But in the meantime, plausible deniability. Don't tell me nothing.

Baybra   What you asking me for then?

Vince   I ain't asked you nothing, I'm telling you.

Baybra   What you telling me?

Vince   I told you already.

Baybra   Well, tell me again.

Vince   I don't blame you. That's all. If you did something / then I—

Baybra   Well, I didn't.

Vince   . . . alright. I believe you. (*Beat.*) Besides, you were always smarter than your old man.

Baybra   Say what?

Vince   I'm just saying, your old man held on to too much. Towards the end there, I think he may have just been trying to make up for mistakes. But you only got a small window to do that. See, it's one thing to try and right your wrongs but sometimes that wrong gonna stay wrong and you just gotta keep it moving, Baybra. You gotta move on—a truism indeed, but still worth noting. I know you got enough sense to know that. Look around you, it's you, Tellulah, Vanessa, Avery . . . me, if I count for anything. You got everything you need. *Now* and I mean right motherfucking now is the time for you to move on. And all we can do is just pray whatever is behind us—stays there . . . right?

Baybra   . . . Right.

Scene Three

A few days later. **Tellulah** *is fixing something to eat.* **Baybra** *walks in with* **Avery**, *in one of the best moods we've seen him in.*

Baybra   What's up, sis?

Avery   Hey, Aunt Tellulah!

Tellulah   Hey. What y'all got going on?

Avery   We went to play basketball. Daddy was showing me how to get in someone's head and get that mental advantage.

Baybra   That's right.

Tellulah   Did you show your daddy all the things Uncle Vince taught you?

Baybra   Yeah she showed me and if you ask me he ain't really taught her shit. Just how to slide her feet real good and make a chest pass.

Tellulah   Fundamentals, Baybra. Isn't that why Coach Morton said you never reached your full potential?

Baybra   Coach Morton was a pussy.

Avery   Anyways, we ended up playing some other guy and his kid and we beat them so bad!

Baybra   Kicked they ass good!

Avery   I almost dunked on that little nigga!

Tellulah   Avery! (*To* **Baybra**.) Good job, Baybra.

Baybra   It's just a little shit-talking. Damn.

Tellulah   You going to make it by the stores today?

Baybra   . . . yeah. I've been there pretty much all day, every day. Figured I could hang with Avery a little bit.

Tellulah   No, I get it. I was just asking. Charles' family been breathing down my back. Sending people down there to spy and look around. Just want to make sure I always have someone at one of the stores too.

Baybra   Hey, baby girl, let me talk to your auntie for a second.

Avery   Okay.

She is about to exit the kitchen.

Tellulah   Avery, you hungry? You want this? I lost my appetite.

Avery   I'm starving, thanks Aunt Tellulah.

She takes the plate and leaves. **Tellulah** *is thinking.*

Baybra   What's on your mind?

Tellulah   What ain't?

Baybra ⋅ I hear you. My mind been running a mile a minute too. I'll be alright though. So will you . . . Tulips. My precious little Tulips.

He chuckles a little, he can never call her that without doing so.

Tellulah   Oh here we go. What's up? What's going on?

Baybra   Nothing.

Tellulah ⋅ Mmmm . . .

Baybra   Well, there's something I wanted to talk to you about. It's about the stores.

Tellulah   Please, I don't want to even think about that. Whatever you want to do, get or change just do it.

Baybra   I don't want to change anything. I'm not trying to do anything either. I think you should . . . you know, what I was thinking is you should find someone else.

Tellulah   Someone else?

Baybra   To look over the stores until you know what you want to do. Or until all this shit is settled with Charles' family.

Tellulah   Okay, fine. Tony offered his help. I'll call him back and let him know I can use it. I told you they're trying to take my husband's business and make me look like I can't handle it and you right there helping them. Got me looking like I can't even keep the damn place staffed.

Baybra   It's just . . . I don't even know if Charles would want / me there.

Tellulah   Don't put this on my husband who's not here to speak up for himself. Charles wanted you here. He wanted you working with him.

Baybra   I just don't want to slide in like I own the place now that the nigga's gone.

Tellulah   Whatever helps you sleep at night, Cortland.

Baybra   Cortland?

Tellulah   Yeah, that's your name. Oh, I'm not calling you Baybra anymore. You ain't been him in a long time.

Baybra   Well, I'm not the only one who's changed. That's for sure. You've been hanging off Charles and under this thumb so long I can hardly remember the real you. Look at you! Today's the first time in I don't know how long that I ain't saw you with all that garbage on your face. Dressing like you somebody you ain't. But you can't fool me. I see through you. (*Beat.*) Talking about Charles wanted me here. The question is why didn't you.

Tellulah   I did want you here.

Baybra   Bullshit.

Tellulah   Believe what you want but I wanted you here. You're all I have from long ago that I can look back on and smile about. I don't have no pictures or dolls or teddy bears. I got my baby brother. We stood in a lot of dark places together. Just us. Reassuring one another there was light coming. And soon. But you ain't looking for the light no more. You just want to sit down in a cold, damp spot and remind me how dark it is. But I don't need reminding. So when you can't provide comfort any longer, then it doesn't make sense to drag you along with me. You're too big now. I can't hold your hand. It doesn't look right. So I gotta put you up, Baybra. Stuff you in my closet. I outgrew you. I'll reminisce about you. Look back on you and smile but you can't tag along. If that means I've changed then I changed. You're right. But I have a life and it doesn't have to include you if you don't want to get in where you fit in. I don't need you how you think I do. I needed you when I was laid up in a hospital but instead you were serving time for beating some kid's goddamn brains out for stealing . . . what? Fifty bucks out your car? And was it even the right person? Was it worth it? Because that's not the Baybra I grew up with. I don't even see him right now. But I still love you. Still wanted you here. No matter who you were. But you can't accept me the same way. You only want me and you only love me as long as I can be the Tellulah you need me to be.

Baybra   That's not true.

Tellulah   Yeah it is.

Baybra   The first time you came to visit me you sat on the other side of that glass calling me every name in the book. Saying I was out of my mind. Yelling how I done went down the wrong road.

Tellulah   Because you fucked up your life!

Baybra   And I ain't arguing that! Now you're going down the wrong road with Charles, you're fucking up and I'm yelling, I'm begging for you to stop and that's wrong? It's not love? You're being foolish. Running right back to this nigga.

Tellulah   Jesus, Baybra, you're talking about something that happened years ago!

Baybra   Damn shame. After all the shit you talked on Mama and Daddy.

Tellulah   It's different.

Baybra   How?

Tellulah   Because it is.

Baybra   Yeah but it ain't.

Tellulah   Because Charles changed. That's how. I didn't have to give him a thousand chances the same way Mama did Daddy. Daddy never changed. Til the day he died he was the same damn person.

Baybra   So there it is. You didn't give him a thousand chances but it was more than one. How many? Nine hundred? Nine-twenty-three? Huh? How many cheeks did you turn? You only got two. Then what'd you do? Turn around so he could kick you in the ass?

Tellulah   You don't know what you're talking about. Daddy lied to you! He lied! Ask Mama!

Baybra   Of course she'll corroborate anything you say.

She explodes.

Tellulah   HE LIED! (*Beat.*) In a marriage it takes getting several chances. But at least Charles wasn't making the same mistakes.

Baybra   Okay, so he never punched you again . . . but that wouldn't stop him from choking you, right? And then he got to throw shit at you. Spit on you. Hell, there's several ways to skin a cat.

Tellulah   You think that little of me? I would just keep running back to someone like that?

Baybra   . . . yeah. I do.

Tellulah   Well, there it is. (*Beat.*) You know, I think it's time you find somewhere else to stay.

Baybra   . . . fine. You think I need this shit, Tellulah? I ain't ever asked to stay here. I ain't ask for a job. I gotta million ways to make a little money. That ain't changed.

Tellulah   Make a little money how? What you up to, huh? I knew you was out there up to no good.

Baybra   And what you care? (*Beat.*) Avery! Come on, baby girl.

Tellulah   She don't need to be going anywhere with you if you going out there to get into some shit.

Avery *enters.*

Baybra   She'll go where I tell her.

Tellulah   It don't work that way, Baybra. (*To* **Avery**.) Avery, baby, go back in there and watch TV or something. I'll take you back to your mama later.

Baybra   She came with me and she'll leave with me. You think I'm going to let you come between me and my daughter just because you mad?

Tellulah   It ain't about me being mad. You're up to no good. (*Beat.*) Go on back in there, Avery.

Baybra   No, come on, let's go, Avery. Like I said.

Avery   Daddy, maybe I / should just—

Baybra   Goddammit I said let's go!

Avery *is unnerved.* **Tellulah** *stands her ground. There seems to be some regret on* **Baybra**'s *part. There's a moment that passes.*

Baybra   Alright . . . yeah, alright . . . cool.

He exits.

Scene Four

Tellulah, Vince, and Vanessa are in the middle of a conversation, discussing the several papers scattered about the kitchen table and island. Tellulah's nerves are bad.

Vince   There's nothing in there, Tellulah.

Tellulah   Maybe there is.

Vanessa   Tellulah, girl, just calm down.

Tellulah   Damn it! You all aren't telling me anything good. What's my options?

Vince   From what I can tell, and I ain't no lawyer, sis, but you don't have many. The contract seems to be saying what you thought it did. Charles' folks gave him the business under the stipulation that it stays within their family in the event he chooses not to run them. He still gets his percentage though and, being his wife, that makes it your money as much as his. It's just a smaller piece than if he was still running the business.

Vanessa   What about the will, though? You said Charles willed the business to Tellulah.

Vince   Yeah, and I had my boy Mike take a look at it. He said the will is a loophole and something worth pursuing but it's still a long shot because it's only executed in the event Charles passed away.

Tellulah   So we'll declare him dead. And when he comes back we'll do whatever we gotta do at that point.

Vince   That requires a death certificate and that'll be hard to come by. I asked Mike about that too. Where's the body? No suspicious circumstances. He wasn't last seen doing anything detrimental to his health. No money problem. No drug problems. Nothing.

Tellulah   You tell me all this shit your boy Mike said, is he a lawyer?

Vince   He's the H.R. rep at the fire department. But he's got a couple years of law school.

Tellulah   So he's not even a damn lawyer?!

Vince   Neither am I. So I don't even know why you got me look through all this shit.

Tellulah   Hell, I don't know either. Cause you ain't helped shit. Talking about no suspicious circumstances. What about being missing for six months? Huh? That ain't nothing.

Vanessa   Listen, we all have to calm down.

Vince   Six months ain't shit. It takes seven years to declare death in absentia. You can thank Mike for that little bit of info. Otherwise, niggas leave their wives every damn day, Tellulah.

Vanessa   Vince!

He calms down. He went too far.

Vince   Look, I'm sorry, alright? Tellulah, without Charles here, the business is probably going back to his family. You need to be prepared for that.

Tellulah   Shit! (*Beat.*) His family want to act like I can't take care of things. Not a single one of them has ever lifted a finger to help out since we took it over. They just been waiting like a dog at the dinner table for something to fall down. (*Beat.*) Did either of you talk to Baybra?

Vince   I did.

Vanessa   So did I.

Tellulah   And?

Vanessa   He doesn't know anything.

Tellulah   Bullshit.

Vince   I don't think he does, Tellulah.

Tellulah   BULLSHIT! That's alright. I shouldn't have asked you for nothing. I'll talk to him.

Vanessa *is simply trying to organize the scattered papers and put them back in old boxes when she comes across something. She looks at it for a while. Then she stares at* **Tellulah**. *Finally,* **Tellulah** *notices.*

Vanessa   Tellulah . . . is this . . . a sonogram?

Tellulah   . . . listen, it's not what you think.

Vanessa   I think it's a sonogram. And if it isn't then what the hell is it?

Tellulah   . . .

Vanessa   Tellulah?

Vince   Yo, let's just put everything back and talk about this all later. Everybody's stressed right now.

Vanessa   No, I want to talk about it right now. (*To* **Tellulah**.) Tellulah?!

Tellulah   I can have something for myself! Okay? I don't have to tell you or anyone else every damn thing.

Vanessa   Wow. Okay, Tellulah. (*Beat.*) Baybra was right.

Tellulah   And just what the hell was Baybra right about, Vanessa?

Vanessa   Everything.

Baybra *enters from back door without knocking. Immediately sensing the tension.*

Baybra   Am I interrupting something?

Vanessa   Nothing at all. I need to pick up Avery from school.

She crosses towards **Baybra** *as she's about to leave.*

Vanessa   Couldn't see the forest for the trees, remember? You were right. So if you did do something, I hope you burned every damn tree down.

She leaves.

Tellulah   Vanessa!

Vince   I'm going to make sure she's cool. I'll catch you all later.

He also crosses towards door and stops near **Baybra**.

You doing alright?

Baybra   Yeah. You?

Vince   Yeah.

Baybra   Cool.

Vince *exits without any other interaction with* **Baybra**.

Tellulah   Baybra, how you doing?

Baybra   Oh, I'm Baybra again? Not Cortland?

Tellulah   I was just trying to piss you off. I hated saying it more than you hated hearing it.

Baybra   I got your text saying to come over. So, here I am.

Tellulah   Where you been staying?

Baybra   With a friend.

Tellulah   With a woman?

Baybra   They just so happen to be a woman, yes.

Tellulah   Well, that's nice. And what about Vanessa?

Baybra   What about her?

Tellulah   Hell, if you don't know I sure don't. Here, have a seat. Want a drink?

Baybra   Sure.

Tellulah *grabs a bottle of something, maybe something* **Baybra** *left behind or her own hidden stash and pours them both a drink.*

Tellulah   I'll be honest, Baybra, I'm tired. Everything that's going on, I'm just tired. So, it's time for us to get back to being us. I'm willing to trade you a truth for a truth.

Baybra   What was Vanessa talking about?

Tellulah   Oh I said *a* truth. As in one. That's the truth you want?

Baybra   I'm not doing all that. I just asked a question. What's wrong with Vanessa?

Tellulah   She was helping me sort out some papers and came across a sonogram.

Baybra *wants to ask more but he knows that was a freebie.*

Baybra   Alright. I'll play your little game.

Tellulah   There ain't a woman God ever made that could take Charles from me. There's nothing more interesting to him. There ain't nothing that could run him away either. So he ain't somewhere and able to come home and simply not coming. And it just so happens to be that I'm looking at you at the same time I can't find him. Odd ain't it? (*Beat.*) What happened to my husband, baby brother?

Baybra   . . . Last time I saw him, we were right here actually.

He is near whatever spot he was at when he last saw **Charles** *and put the gun to his head.* **Charles** *slowly emerges and gets back in the same position he was in when* **Baybra** *had the gun to his head. It looks exactly as it did only* **Baybra** *is narrating it to his sister.*

Baybra   I put a gun to his head cause a motherfucker like that thinks he's smarter than everyone else. Thinks his lies are too intelligent for my limited understanding. A loaded gun is like a translator.

He now is back completely with **Charles***, giving him all his attention. They are in that moment again.*

Baybra   Shut your ass up! And tell me the truth! Don't open your mouth to say nothing but the truth! I swear to God, Charles, I ain't playing with you no more!

Charles   Alright! Alright! Baybra . . . I'll tell you. She—she—she . . . you know, was pregnant, man. Okay? That much is true. And she lost the baby but listen to me, it wasn't because of me.

Baybra   Yeah it was! What the fuck you do? Beat her for gaining weight? For being tired? What you do, Charles?

Charles *is wobbly.*

Charles   I need to sit down. I need some water, man.

Baybra   You ain't that damn old. You gonna stand up, like a man, nigga.

Charles   Come on, Baybra, let me . . . let me . . . let me get some water at least.

Baybra   Nah! You can die of thirst for all I care. Now, keep talking you cotton-mouth motherfucker. What else?

Charles   That's it. That's the truth. She lost the baby about four months into it and here we are.

Baybra   That's all we ever talked about. You know that? Having some kids. Three or four apiece. Having big ass dinners on the holidays. Being a family. Doing shit the right way. And you took that from her. But let me guess, you blame her, don't you? How many times you beat her for it?

Charles   Baybra /

Baybra   How many times while I was locked up did you put your hands on her? Slap her, punch her, choke her, stomp her? How many times you call her out her name? Threaten her? How many?

Charles   What do you want me to say, Baybra?

Baybra   Bitch nigga! You flunk kindergarten or something? *What do I want you to say*?! I asked you how many, give me a goddamn number!

Charles   Baybra, we just keep going around / and around—

Baybra   You know what? It doesn't really matter. I was never gonna let you get away with any of it. Whether it was just once or a hundred times after that.

Charles   What you saying, Baybra? (*Beat.*) Lord God . . .

Baybra   *Lord God* what? Lord God sent me! I'm his vengeance in the flesh. (*Beat.*) You love her don't you?

Charles   Yeah I love her. More than life itself.

Baybra   That's what I wanted to hear. Tell me something, how would you do it?

Charles   What?

Baybra   You said you thought about killing yourself. How would you do it? You ain't really thought about it if you didn't come up with at least part of the plan?

Charles   That old steel bridge can't nobody use anymore, that sits over the river—I use to go there and drink and smoke with some fellas long time ago. At nighttime, it sits over that water and the water is black and shiny, looks like if you fell into it you would just keep falling forever. If I was ever going to do it, I'd stand at that bridge with my arms held out and just drop face first. Gotta be about two hundred feet. Smacking the water alone would probably break every bone in my body and I'd just sink and drown. I figured if I allowed myself that much torture then maybe, just maybe I'd be forgiven.

Baybra   Hell yeah. Now we're talking. I think you got a damn good plan, brother Charles. Shit, I know I could forgive you. Yeah, that would earn my forgiveness. So when you going?

Charles   What? We talking about what a motherfucker thinks about, not what I'm actually gonna do.

Baybra   So that was all talk?

Charles   You asked me how and I told you how. But I ain't doing no crazy shit like that.

Baybra   Okay well then I'll just do it. Right here. Right now. You'll be dead. I'll go to prison. She'll lose us both but she'll move on. I'll do anything for her. Would you?

Charles *is breathing heavy. He's scared. He's giving in.*

Charles   So this is it? Like this? You got this in you? You're a killer?

Baybra   Nah, I ain't no killer. And nobody's going to think I'm one either. See, I'll tell them I had to do it. *He's been mistreating my sister* . . . that's what I'll tell them. *Beating her. Cheating. A different woman every night.* Hell, maybe I'll tell them how I seen you hugging Avery just a little too tight. She's young, she can be easily manipulated.

Charles   You a motherfucking lie! You hear me? You ol' worthless ass nigga!

He has stood up and rushed **Baybra***, catching him off guard. He begins to choke* **Baybra** *who in return chokes him back, finally throwing him across the floor.* **Charles** *is no longer a match for* **Baybra***.*

Baybra   This is what she wants, Charles. She told me. She feels like she could live if you were gone.

Charles   Why can't I just leave? Just . . . let me walk away.

Baybra   Because it ain't good enough. You're weak man. You'd try and come back. Now, wouldn't you?

Charles *weeps. He carries a lot of weight.*

Charles   Fuck it . . . I'll do it.

Baybra   You'll do it?

Charles   Yeah . . . I'm . . . I'm . . . I'm gonna do it.

Baybra   Nah, I don't believe you.

Charles   Why not? What I got to live for? You say Tellulah don't want me? This is what she wants? She confided in you?

Baybra   I swear it to you, big brother. But this'll prove it to her, that you love her. That you'd do better if you could.

Charles   Don't leave me out there. Let me get buried by my mama and daddy at least, Baybra. Tell 'em where to find me.

Baybra   Alright.

Charles   Give me your word.

Baybra   . . . you got my word.

Charles *heads for the door.*

Charles   I'm praying for you, Baybra. May God rescue you from this illness, man. From all this hate and unforgiveness. And if you ever look back and wonder . . . yes, baby brother, I forgive you too.

He leaves. **Tellulah** *stands there crushed, in denial. It's her and* **Baybra** *again.*

Tellulah   So, he probably is just staying away. Waiting for you to leave before he comes home. That's all. He—he—he wouldn't have done that. Couldn't have. He's just waiting it out.

Baybra   Yeah, maybe.

Tellulah   Did you look for my husband? Did you check? Did you see him?

Baybra   Nah. I figured maybe he did it or maybe he didn't. Either way he ain't come back. You free, sis.

No longer in denial, she knows he's not coming back.

Tellulah   He wouldn't be out there somewhere and not at least call me! He'd have come home! You gave him your word that you'd send someone. You gave him your word!

Baybra   And he gave me his a long time ago before he *did what he did* and it didn't mean shit. So I owed him one good lie.

Tellulah   You self-righteous son of a bitch!

Baybra   But I was right, wasn't I? I had to be. Why else would he do something like this? How many times he jump on you? I want to hear you say it.

Tellulah   I don't care what you want.

Baybra   I give you a truth, you give me a truth.

Tellulah   I'm not giving you shit. All I've ever done was give you. But all you want is someone to feel sorry for you. Poor ol' Baybra. Yeah you've had bad breaks but you've had good things too. You just never wanted them cause you wouldn't have any more excuses. Now you want to take my good things! You ain't shit and I ain't got shit else for you!

She slaps him. He takes it. She slaps him again.

Baybra   I never expected you to say thank you. Don't need you to. But the motherfucker came between us, Tellulah. If he gonna do that he gotta make life better for you and he didn't. He had to go, understand?

Tellulah   I don't understand a fucking / thing!

Baybra   Whether you believe it or not, your life still bleeds over into mine. So if you dying, even just a little, I'm dying, sis. You can't see that? If you bleeding, I'm bleeding.

Tellulah   Just shut up.

Baybra   If he hitting you, he hitting me and I ain't gonna let no nigga smack me in the mouth!

Tellulah   Goddammit shut up! Shut the hell up! (*Beat.*) You're so good, Baybra. Ain't you? So good at making things what you want them to be. Making people believe you're all about them.

Laughs—incredulously and ironically.

In a past life you sold snake oil by the gallons, nigga. You must've. Then you sell my husband some lie about what I say or think or feel. But here's the real truth, you oughta hear what I say about you. See, I could live if you were gone. You the only thing I've ever been shackled to. Charles was a choice. Daddy's dead. Mama don't want you. Vince don't need you. Vanessa and Avery would be so much better without having to disrupt their lives just to squeeze you in somewhere. And I love you, Baybra, but I don't know for how much longer. Let me keep loving you and get the fuck out of my life. Be the man he was.

She pulls a gun from the drawer and offers it to him.

Baybra   Is that what you want, Tellulah? Is it? / Cause I don't need no convincing.

Tellulah   You damn right!

Baybra   I'll do the shit right here, right now. All for you. / See, I'm the one who really loves you, Tellulah.

Tellulah   Then do it goddammit!

Baybra   . . . what you gonna have left, sis?

A fear comes over him. If not fear, something we haven't seen on him yet. He paces around and contemplates leaving the house but doesn't. He finishes off his drink he poured earlier and stands in clear view of her. Then he puts the gun to his head. It seems like a lifetime but it's only a brief moment and then he pulls the trigger . . . but it doesn't go off. He lets out a scream but then heavy breathing when he realizes it didn't shoot. He believes this was a test. That **Tellulah** *never intended for it to go off; however,* **Tellulah** *knows something he doesn't, that it should've fired.* **Baybra** *goes to place the gun on the island, tossing it almost and as it lands it then goes off loud and clear.* **Tellulah** *screams and* **Baybra** *is in shock. He is not hit and gives himself a onceover to ensure that he isn't. He tries his best not to be fazed by this, not to be hurt by this, but ultimately he is destroyed. After a moment, he drops to his knees.* **Tellulah** *rushes to him and consoles him as he sobs into her waist.*

Tellulah   Shhhh . . . shhh . . . come on now. It's alright. Okay? I'm right here.

Blackout.

The end.

Begetters

No one person is solely responsible for
where they are nor who they are.
We are inspired, influenced, and molded.
All we can do is show grace for those
who placed us on this road
and ask for grace from those
whom we'll place one day.
Because the shit isn't easy and love is hardly ever enough.

Begetters received its world premiere on May 13, 2022, at KC Melting Pot Theatre in Kansas City, Missouri with the following cast:

Spicer	Harvey Williams
Norma	Lynn King
Gordon	Lewis Morrow
Kiko	E. Larry Guidry
Andrea	Jacquelyn Price
Anita	Amber Redmond-Harrah
Dr. Ross	Cecilia Ananya

Director	Ile Haggins
Set Design	Doug Schroeder
Lighting Design	Warren Deckert
Sound Design	Dennis Jackson
Costume Design	Markeyta L. Young
Stage Manager	Theodore "Priest" Hughes
Assistant Stage Manager	Desmond "337" Jones

Characters

Spicer *(sixties), man, Black*
Norma *(sixties), woman, Black*
Gordon *(thirties), man, Black*
Kiko *(thirties), man, Black*
Anita *(twenties), woman, Black*
Dr. Ross *(fifties or so), woman, Black*
Andrea *(thirties), woman, Black*

Setting

Therapist's office.

Time

2020.

Slash (/) indicates overlapping dialogue and where the next line should begin
Ellipsis (. . .) indicates searching for words more than just space or pause

The Black characters are speaking in Black vernacular—not to be confused with illiteracy or lack of education. For the most part, words aren't misspelled to indicate this. If an actor is struggling with this, they've probably been miscast.

Scene One

Inside a therapist's office. It's nice, yet simple. A small and artsy table is somewhere in the room. On it—some candles, tissue, and a small plant. Feng shui shit really. Most notably, however? A rather large rock, something that would require two hands to lift. It could be art, but honestly? It just looks like a rock. The lighting is just right, provided by the ultra-sleek lamps and blinds opened to just the right degree. Get the picture? This is the type of room you'd want to pour your heart out in. In this room we find **Norma** *and* **Spicer**. *A married couple. As the lights come up,* **Spicer** *is far more impatient than* **Norma**. *Neither happy to be there though. She's holding a clipboard and reading over something. He's looking around, taking it in, waiting; finally he speaks.*

Spicer   It's cold as hell in here. Why they keep it so cold? They wanna freeze your damn secrets out of you. I hope they plan on turning the air down.

Norma   Why would they turn the air down if you're cold?

Spicer   Turn it down, turn it up, do something with it. Make it warm. Shit. You know what I mean.

Norma   Just clarifying.

Spicer   You ain't cold?

Norma   I'm fine. It feels good in here to me.

Spicer   Well, then, whenever you're fine I'm cold, ain't I?

Norma   When aren't you cold? I could be convulsing from having a damn heat stroke and you'd still be there saying it was cold.

Spicer   Because you've convulsed . . .

Norma   Oh I've convulsed.

Spicer   Yeah, alright. (*Grunts.*) I tell you what though, she need a decorator in here. She just putting up any damn thing.

Norma   Whatchu know about decorating, Spicer?

He notices the large rock.

Spicer   I know a big goddamn rock ain't no decoration. She probably paid a thousand bucks for that thing. I could've gotten her all the rocks she wanted for a hundred. Put 'em in my truck and dumped them right in here for her.

Norma   Maybe that one's special. Maybe she use it to bust somebody upside the head when they keep talking shit.

Spicer   Well, she got the right rock for it.

He continues to fuss and sigh and grunt.

We could've done this at our house if she was just going to leave us in here with a form to fill out. Mailed it back to her ass.

Norma   She'll be back. It's just an exercise. To get us to open up. You can't give anyone a straight answer. You don't trust nobody. I think it's a good idea. If you won't talk to her, talk to me.

Spicer   I talk to you all the time. What difference has it made? We still ended up here.

Norma   And I talk to you but not like this. We haven't asked these questions. To each other or to ourselves. I haven't anyways. Maybe we need a little direction.

Spicer   Well, fuck it then, come on with it. Ask me.

Norma   Or do you want to ask me the questions first?

Spicer   Norma, just come on with it. I don't care who goes first. You got the questions already, you go.

Norma   Alright.

Reads over the clipboard one last time.

What's the very last thing you said to your son?

Spicer (*triggered, he represses it though*)   I don't know. I umm . . . I think we were talking about / something and—

Norma   Spicer, what's the last thing you said to your son?

Spicer   He was over the house and he had just moved that new mattress in for us. We had talked a little bit and / you and I were—

Norma   But what was the last thing you said to him?

Spicer   I'm getting there.

Norma   It says we need to be able to simply answer the questions. Backstory is just another way to be evasive.

Spicer   Norma, you ain't the damn doctor.

Norma   I'm just reading what the woman wrote.

She shows him clipboard as proof.

What was the very last thing you said to him?

Spicer   I asked him what you said about the oxtails. Alright?! The motherfucking oxtails. I asked him—*what your mama say about the oxtails?*

Then suddenly, **Gordon** *and* **Kiko** *pull a large and bulky mattress across the stage.* **Spicer** *and* **Norma** *look on.*

Gordon   Ey don't drag it. Pick that joint up.

Kiko   What the hell your folks need a bed this big for?

Gordon   Hell if I know. Same reason anybody needs a big bed. Maybe they're wild sleepers.

Kiko   Or they have some wild sex.

Gordon   Hey, if so, power to 'em. We should all be so lucky.

Kiko   Oh, I've been very lucky.

Gordon   Yeah, sure. Just pick up the bed.

Kiko   Wait . . . Erica's withholding?

Gordon   Things are . . . you know. . . *shaky*.

Kiko   No progress?

Gordon   Progress is a process, my brother.

Spicer *approaches the two.*

Spicer   How y'all coming? Y'all ain't got it in the room yet?

Gordon   It ain't in the room if it's right here in front of you, Pops.

Spicer   It ain't that heavy. I used to move shit two or three times heavier than that.

Kiko   Not heavier than this, you didn't.

Spicer   Heavier, bigger, and with less places to grip it at. I had the same mattress before, same damn model, and I moved it by myself.

Kiko   You want my end then, Mr. Jones?

Spicer   Get your narrow ass out the way. I'll get it.

He makes no attempt to get it.

Ask your mama all the shit I used to move.

Gordon   Where is Mama?

Spicer   Back there making some cake for Reverend Murphy. That no good ass nigga.

Kiko   What's wrong with Reverend Murphy? He baptized me.

Spicer   Shit. Motherfucking Bernie Madoff must be handling your stocks and bonds then.

Gordon   Come on, man, please don't get my old man started on Reverend Murphy. Let's get this mattress out the way.

They drag the mattress off stage, presumably to a bedroom somewhere. **Norma** *approaches* **Spicer** *while on the phone. She speaks to him while holding the phone away and speaking so only he hears her and not the person on the other end.*

Norma   Did you make some coffee or not?

Spicer   I asked if you wanted some but you didn't answer me. I won't make a whole pot if you don't want some. But I don't want you sipping from mine either. I want my coffee.

Norma's attention is back to her phone conversation.

Norma   Hey! Yes, I'm still here Reverend Murphy. Yes, it's all ready for you and I can't wait for you to see it. You'll love it.

Spicer   You want some coffee or not?

She waves him off. He starts to walk away and she snaps her fingers to get his attention.

Norma   Matter fact, make a pot. I can fix my own cup though. You put too much damn sugar in it. (*Back on phone.*) No I'm still here! (*Beat.*) Okay, see you then. (*Beat.*) Oh please, glad to do it. (*Beat.*) Alright, bye bye.

Spicer   I told you I don't want you waiting hand and foot on Reverend Murphy's ass. I don't like it.

Norma   Ain't nobody waiting on him hand and foot. The man been at the church twenty-five years and we're commemorating it. That's all. Did Gordon get that bed in?

Spicer   Commemorate me if you wanna commemorate something. Shit. Is he your husband?

Norma   What?

Spicer   I said is he your husband? I don't like you running all over town, planning, spending money, fetching all type of shit, and baking cakes for this nigga.

Norma   Hey that's enough now! He's our pastor.

Spicer   Nah, he's *your* pastor. He ain't nobody to me but Clarence. The same nigga who owes me fifteen hundred dollars for the Buick I sold him in '97.

Norma   How he owe it to you? We were planting a seed.

Spicer   We ain't plant shit! You all wanted him to preach full time so you could call him all hours of the day with your problems. And that's fine. But he ain't ask me for a seed. He asked me for money. For a loan. Which I obliged. Now all of a sudden everyone is saying he don't owe them nothing and that's fine too. But you all ain't give him fifteen hundred dollars. Y'all donated a couple suits and a nice chair for the pulpit. Thrift shop shit. I got his ass a car. What I did and what everyone else did don't compare. You act like you can't see that. He came to me man to man and asked me if I could help him out. And I'm telling you it wasn't no damn seed.

Norma   Okay, Spicer.

Spicer   Okay, Norma!

Kiko *comes back in.*

Kiko   Hey, Gordon asked what wall you want the bed against?

Norma   Any wall will work.

Kiko   You want it across from the TV though?

Spicer   Man, throw the son of a bitch out the window if you want. Damn the bed. She ain't gonna do nothing but complain about it no how.

Kiko *goes back to the room.*

Norma   You talking about a twenty-year-old loan like it's got you in a bind somehow. You sound stupid.

Spicer   Ey, watch it now. Don't lose yourself.

Norma   What is your problem this morning?

Spicer   I just asked if you wanted some coffee and you shoo me away like I'm some fucking mosquito. I don't like that shit.

Norma   Well, you're irritating me like one.

Spicer   Yeah, alright. Keep on. Let all them divorced, lonely, *ugly* ass women from the church convince you your old ass can find something better. You gonna be disappointed, woman. I can tell you that now.

Norma   Who said anything about finding something better?

Spicer   Well, don't be shooing me away. When I talk to you, listen up goddammit.

Norma   *Listen up*? You really trying to swing your dick around ain't you? Who challenged you, baby? Huh? Who done said you ain't the man you think you are? Cause it wasn't me. I spent all night working on this cake. I got a thousand people calling me asking where it is, what it look like, and if it's finished, and in between all of that I got you asking me if I want some coffee or not cause Lord knows we gotta measure the coffee carefully. We can't dare let one damn grind go to waste.

Spicer   It ain't about it going to waste. Although ain't no need in wasting it if it can be avoided by you simply answering yes or no when I'm talking to you. I ain't trying to walk in the kitchen and fix me some coffee then come all the way back in here only for you to decide now you want some. And then I'm supposed to go get it for you.

Norma   I've gotten you a-many-damn-cups of coffee, Spicer Jones!

Spicer   You a damn chicken woman! I'm a pig. Just cause you give me eggs don't mean I owe you bacon.

Norma   Is that so? Well, you can just go sit your ol' gimp-legged ass down and don't ever offer me another damn cup of coffee. I'll fix it myself. Fuck!

Spicer   See there! You think it's funny. This gout done came down on me and you talking shit. I'll tell you what though, that damn cake is the last thing Reverend Murphy getting from this household.

Norma   He'll get whatever I want him to have.

Spicer   You a lie!

Norma   And you a fool! If I want to bake a cake for somebody, I'll do just that.

Spicer   Not another man, you won't.

Norma   Watch me.

Spicer   Yeah and watch me throw that shit on the floor. Now I said that cake was the last one. Keep talking and I'll go back there and piss in the motherfucker!

Gordon *comes out.*

Gordon   Ey, ey, ey! What are y'all doing? Fussing like this in front of folks. Kiko can hear y'all back there.

Spicer   And? It's our house!

Norma   That's your daddy raising all that hell.

Gordon   It sounded like both of you.

Norma   Well, maybe you oughta stop eavesdropping and move the mattress like we asked.

Gordon   It's moved.

Spicer   Alright then. What I owe you and Kiko?

Gordon   You don't owe us nothing. Wasn't a problem.

Kiko *comes out.*

Kiko   Hey, Mr. Jones, I moved that mirror so it wouldn't be over the headboard. Wouldn't want it dropping on you while you're sleeping . . . or doing *other* things.

Spicer   Gordon said he don't want no money. I know you ain't a big enough fool to turn it down, are you?

Kiko   Your money's no good with me, Mr. Jones.

Spicer   You want something to eat then? Piece of cake? Mrs. Jones made some chocolate cake. Go on and get a piece.

Norma   That's for Reverend Murphy!

Spicer   Somebody gotta taste it to make sure it's alright.

Norma   I made that cake a hundred times. It tastes the same as it always does.

Spicer   And ain't one of them times been for me.

Norma   See . . . I'm done with this. I'm done, man!

She storms off.

Spicer   Be done then. Matter fact! Norma! Hey!

He storms off after her.

Kiko   Damn. They still at it like that?

Gordon   Shit's embarrassing to tell the truth.

Kiko   You ain't gotta be embarrassed in front of me. I know all your secrets. I know about Tasha Alexander.

Gordon   Oh shit! We doing that? I guess I can mention a particular sixty-year-old gym teacher in your freshman year—Ms. Everett.

Kiko   Man she wasn't even forty!

Gordon   Shiiiiitt . . .

Kiko   Well, ey, like Coach Long used to say, ain't no need for secrets or regrets /

Gordon/Kiko   Just lessons learned.

This is a normal routine. They shake hands.

Kiko   You sticking around?

Gordon   Yeah, I'm gonna hang with them a bit. Appreciate the help.

Kiko   Of course. I'll catch up with you. You, Erica, and the kids should come over later. Me and Anita ain't doing nothing. She making some wings and potato skins. We can get on some spades.

Gordon   Sounds good. We'll be there.

Kiko *leaves and we hear* **Norma** *stomping back in—irate.*

Norma   I can't stand your Black ass, Spicer Jones! I swear I can't!

Gordon   Mama, what's wrong?

Norma   I made that cake for Reverend Murphy. A big old beautiful cake. For his twenty-fifth-year celebration and your daddy's nasty, crazy, jealous ass went back there and put his dick all in it. Ruined it!

Gordon   What?

Norma   You heard me! He put his damn dick in the cake!

Spicer *come in, zipping up his pants.*

Spicer   I sure did! I fucked it up . . . literally. Make another one and I'll do it again. I told you stop talking to me any ol' way. Didn't I?

Norma   You're so damn proud. You indignant Black bastard!

Gordon   Can it be fixed?

Norma   Fixed? Fixed how son? You want to eat a dick-filled cake? Huh?

Gordon   . . . no. Can't say that I do.

Norma   You're just unbearable anymore. If Gordon wasn't here I'd throw something at your ass!

She storms out again while **Spicer** *yells after her.*

Spicer   Throw it if you want to. I bet the motherfucker comes right back at you like a damn boomerang. (*To* **Gordon**.) I been good to that woman. You hear me? Too good to be treated any ol' way.

Gordon I hear you, Pops. Can't you be good a little longer though? Y'all too grown to act like this.

Spicer Cause you know what it means to be grown.

Gordon I know it means not putting your dick in a cake.

Spicer Oh is that right huh? It also means not sitting your sorry ass around and letting your woman be the breadwinner.

Gordon What's that got to do with anything?

Spicer Just been on my mind.

Gordon Always the opportunist, huh, Pop?

Spicer Went from me and your mama taking care of you to now your wife. My daddy is spinning in his grave to know one of his grandsons, a descendant, blood of his blood, got his woman bringing home the bacon. What's grown about that?

Gordon Erica makes more than me. Ain't nothing I can do about that.

Spicer Yeah there is. Get you a second job. A third. A damn fourth and fifth. But you can't let no woman wear the pants. *You* asking *her* if you can do this or that. And it's cause as the money goes, so goes the power. That's the way of the world. Not Spicer Jones philosophizing. I ain't no sexist boy. I kept your mama liberated for a long time. You hear me? But the fact remains, I wore the pants.

Gordon So do I.

Spicer Nah you don't. Listen, why you think it's called wearing the pants? Cause back in the day men wore pants and women wore dresses. Back in the day that is. And what you think those pants had? Pockets. And what was in those pockets? A little piece of money. You couldn't just wear some pants and be a man. You had to have some money. That was the point of it all. Money! Moo-lah! Some coin, nigga. You understand?

Gordon I'm following.

Spicer Now I used to cash my check and bring your mama cold hard cash. I put it in her hands. Wads of hundreds and fifties and twenties. She felt the weight of it. I put it in her hand and it must've been a lot cause her hand dropped, you feel me? Me grabbing your mama's titties or ass or giving her a big wet kiss couldn't make her feel nothing like how that money made her feel. Had her ass open like a 7-11 too. Paying these bills with a little extra leftover was her foreplay. You understand what I'm getting at?

Gordon I believe I do.

Spicer I give her the money, she paid the bills, put some away for savings, and do whatever she wanted with the rest. And look at us, forty years strong.

Gordon Forty years strong? Pops, you in here fucking a cake and she acts like she wants to kill you cause of it.

Spicer   Yeah . . . I might've overreacted. But man your mama burn me up sometimes. She always had a mouth on her.

Gordon   Yeah, she does.

Spicer   Whoa! Whoa! Whoa! Hold on now. I'll smack the shit outta you! That's your mama you talking about. My wife.

Gordon   I was just agreeing with you.

Spicer   Well, agree respectfully. I don't play that shit. (*Beat.*) It was a good-looking cake though. You can go on in there and get a piece. Damn what she talking about. I ain't put my dick but on one side.

Gordon   I don't have to explain to you why I'm not going to do that, right?

Spicer   Listen, man, while I got you. I been meaning to talk to you.

Gordon   Alright.

Spicer   I think your mama going crazy. I ain't talking about getting a little silly in her older years. I'm talking about crazy. She forgetting shit. She don't understand a damn thing I tell her.

Gordon   What's happened?

Spicer   Take the other day for instance. I wanted a big pot of oxtail stew. I brought home a good three or four pounds of the oxtails. Set them on the counter so they could thaw out. We had already talked about it. I go lay down for a bit. I wake up to something smelling good in the kitchen. I open the pot, take me a fork, and try to pull one of those oxtails out. Can't find nan one. This woman done made some vegetable soup basically. I ask her where the oxtails are and she said *what oxtails. You ain't bring no oxtails home.*

Gordon   What happened to the oxtails?

Spicer   Brother, are you listening to me?! That's what I'm saying. I don't know what the fuck happened to the oxtails.

Gordon   So y'all were going to have oxtails . . .

Spicer   That's right.

Gordon   You bought the oxtails . . .

Spicer   Damn straight. Spent fifty bucks on 'em.

Gordon   But she ain't cook them.

Spicer   Bingo.

Gordon   She says she didn't see them.

Spicer   Trying to say I ain't even buy them!

Gordon   Here's what I want to know—why didn't she ever ask you where the oxtails were if you talked about it already? Why'd she just make the stew?

Spicer   That's what I'm . . . boy I oughta slap you! Thank you! Now you see me. You see what I'm saying? She knew good and well we never talked about no vegetable stew.

Gordon   How was the stew though?

Spicer   Don't fuck with me, son.

Gordon   My bad. Alright, well, I guess I can talk to her. I don't know what I'm supposed to say though.

Spicer   Just feel her out. See if she all there.

Gordon   Okay. But if I can't /

Spicer   Norma! Your son wanna talk to you! Norma!

Norma *enters.*

Norma   What's going on?

Spicer   Gordon wants to talk to you. I'm going to get me something to drink.

He leaves.

Norma   Hey, baby. What's wrong?

Gordon   Nothing's wrong. I just wanted to talk to you. Not about anything in particular. We just haven't talked one-on-one in a while.

Norma   A while? Did we ever?

Gordon   Didn't we?

Norma   Not to my recollection. But I welcome it.

Gordon   So, how you feeling, Mama?

Norma   I feel alright. My back's been hurting. But your daddy's crippled ass been walking around like he's a paraplegic.

Gordon   Paraplegics can't walk, can they?

Norma   Don't be a smart ass all your life. You know what I'm saying. He been fussing and crying about his gout so much I can't dare mention anything is wrong with me. He sucking all the pity out the room for himself.

Gordon   I can go take you to see a doctor about your back.

Norma   No, I'll be alright. Your daddy is the one you need to be concerned about and not because of his gout.

Gordon   Oh yeah? What's going on—his blood pressure?

Norma   He's losing his damn mind. That's what. Listen, did I tell you about the oxtails?

Gordon   Nah . . . *you* haven't said anything about the oxtails.

Norma   Well /

We hear **Spicer** *yelling as he emerges.*

Spicer   Norma! Why the hell you throw all that cake away?

Norma   What?! What kind of fool are you? Asking me why I threw it away.

Spicer   That big ass cake. All you had to do was cut that end off. You ain't about to spend another six hours messing up the kitchen. Measuring, mixing, pouring, and baking another cake for that man!

Norma   I'll do as I damn well please, Spicer.

Spicer   Listen here you big head ass woman! I'll /

Gordon   Ey! Can you two just chill? At least while I'm here? You ain't gotta do this shit in front of me all the damn time. I know you like an audience but I've seen this show before. Several times over. I don't want to watch it no more. I'm tired of watching. Just let me leave and then you can argue and fuss and fight and tear the damn house down if you want.

Spicer   Oh this boy just talks to us however he wants, don't he?

Norma   He sure does.

Spicer   He must want to get that ass bent over. I still got an ass whooping or two left in me. Who you think you're talking to?

Gordon   It's getting old. I'm tired of seeing this. Ain't cute no more. And you've been doing it in front of my kids too. If you were hoping I didn't know—I do. I want you to cut that shit out.

Spicer   *Your* kids? *Our* grandbabies, man!

Norma *pulls out the dramatics; patronizingly.*

Norma   Oh, well we're so sorry, son. So sorry this is just an unfit place for your kids. That it was so unfit for you growing up. Okay? We're so goddamn sorry.

Gordon   See, can't nobody tell y'all nothing. Including one another. You can't tell him and he can't tell you shit. Let alone anyone else.

Spicer   Ey, you better watch that mouth, boy.

Norma   Something's gotten into you, Gordon. I'm not gonna stand here while you try to purge yourself of whatever the hell it is.

She returns to the couch, a patient in the therapist's office once again.

Spicer   You know I ain't going to stand for that. You go in there and apologize to your mother.

Gordon *looks at his father long and hard. He heads for the door.*

Spicer   Hey, boy! You hear what I said?! What I tell you to do?

Gordon *keeps walking and then* **Spicer** *yells for him again in a different way. Less demanding. Seems like an apology.*

Spicer   Gordon, hold on, son . . .

Gordon *turns around.*

Spicer   What'd your mama say about the oxtails?

Gordon *can't believe it. He leaves.* **Spicer** *returns to the couch as well. His wife looks at him. He can't even look back at her.*

Spicer   I asked him about the oxtails. That's the very last thing I said to him. My son.

Scene Two

In the black, we hear a scream of despair and hurt and disbelief. It's a woman screaming—it was **Norma**. *As the lights come up we see a visibly shaken* **Kiko** *in whatever he would sleep in standing far across from* **Norma**. *He is still and looks as if he has just seen a ghost.* **Anita** *stands by.* **Norma** *is wearing what she had on from the previous scene. This is a flashback.* **Spicer** *remains on the couch.* **Norma** *is looking at* **Kiko** *and* **Anita**, *listening to them as if she were there but she doesn't get closer, just observes with a million tons of hurt weighing her down.*

Anita   Baby? Who you talking to? It's five a.m.

Kiko   That was Mrs. Jones—Gordon's mama. I let her know the police just came by here.

Anita   The police? Everything okay?

Kiko   Nah. Ain't shit okay. Shit ain't never gonna be okay again.

Anita   Baby you're scaring me.

Kiko (*struggling to get this out*)   They uh . . . the police . . . couldn't reach Gordon's folks . . . guess he had me down as next of kin. They just told me . . . Gordon and Erica are dead.

Anita   What?! Hold on, Kiko, wh-what are you saying?!

Kiko   There was a shooting at Erica's job. Gordon was there dropping her off for whatever reason. Somebody came in and shot the place up. Just hunting motherfuckers down.

Anita *now shares* **Kiko**'s *shock.*

Anita   Oh my God. Kiko . . . baby don't tell me this. What about the babies?

Kiko   They wasn't with them. (*Beat.*) That's a call I ain't ever want to make to nobody. Let alone about the only nigga I ever considered a brother. My man is gone, baby. Fuck! He's gone.

As she consoles him, **Norma** *begins to speak. Soon thereafter* **Kiko** *and* **Anita** *disappear.*

Norma   And it's not a call he should've had to make. (*To* **Spicer**.) But you and I had been fighting. Going at it non-stop. Going strong. I was tired of it. So I just left the house and I turned my phone off. I missed my baby trying to miss your ass. And you? You just flat out wouldn't answer your phone. At least you heard it ringing. If not, you had to hear them knocking at the door.

Spicer   I ain't hear nothing! / I ain't hear a damn thing!

Norma   You just decided not to answer.

Spicer   Don't do that! Having it on but not answering it ain't no worse than turning it off so you don't have to hear it ring. You not being there ain't no different than me not hearing them knock. Why you wanna make one more right than the other? Make me more wrong than you?

Norma   Cause you always deferring to me! Even when he was a kid. *Ask your mama. Go tell your mama.* The school calls and you tell them they gotta speak with his mama. And you weren't doing nothing.

Spicer   I was working goddammit!

Norma   You can work and do other things sometimes, Spicer. Fulfill your duty as a husband and father. You can work and talk. Not all the time. But sometimes. You could've taken a call here and there. But you never did. And you didn't that morning either. Couldn't even answer the door. They had to track down Kiko. And how many times I beg you to clear your voicemails? You had a hundred saved up so they couldn't even leave you nothing. I got stuck with the voicemails.

Spicer   You act like I didn't have to hear it! I listened to it. It's in my head playing over and over too. Every damn day just like it's doing you.

Gordon *emerges. He stands away from his parents. As he talks, he's scared but he tries to hide it.*

Gordon   Mama . . . listen, it's uh . . . it's me, Mama. Some shit is going down. I'm up here at Erica's job and . . . I just want you to know I love you and Pops. You hear me? I love y'all. I know we ain't talked in a few days . . .

We hear gunfire and screams.

Jesus! Look, I ain't mad. I just been busy. But I'll be there Sunday for dinner . . . alright? I'm gonna make sure we get over there Sunday. And we gonna laugh about the cake and the oxtails and everything else.

He's trying to laugh but it's hard to fake it.

Mama, I love you. Tell the old man the same.

He walks off. **Spicer** *and* **Norma** *return to the couch and* **Dr. Ross** *enters and takes her seat.*

Dr. Ross   How are we coming along?

Spicer   You've thrown a real wrench in my shit, doc. That's the truth. I was making strides and you done thrown a wrench, a hurdle, a fucking banana peel in front of me. I don't see how none of this helps at all.

Dr. Ross   And Norma, do you feel the same? Do you question the effectiveness or usefulness of our sessions?

Norma   I really don't know.

Dr. Ross   Well, here's what I know—you two have difficulties talking. I suspect you don't talk much about these things to one another, therefore the chances of you talking to me are pretty slim. So, these exercises are just to knock some rust off. Get you opening up just a little. Get you communicating amongst yourselves and then hopefully with me. Then I can help you process some of your feelings and thoughts regarding losing your son and daughter-in-law. Baby steps. That's all it is.

Norma   We were just talking about the last time Gordon called us. Called me. The voicemail he left.

Dr. Ross   The day of the shooting?

Norma   Yes. But we didn't get to the phone. Because I was trying to prove something to Spicer and he was trying to prove something to me.

Dr. Ross   Prove what?

Norma   I guess how much we don't give a damn. I wanted him to know I could not give a damn just as much as he could. But it got proved to the wrong person that day.

Dr. Ross   Perhaps that wasn't what Gordon was left thinking about. I doubt he felt as if you two didn't *give a damn* in that moment—based on the content of the voicemail.

Norma   You can measure love, Dr. Ross. People like to say you can't but you can. You measure it by the things you do for someone that you know they appreciate. And what you had to sacrifice to do it. Gordon was the sentimental type. Clingy even. He liked to be heard when he talked. He liked to be able to reach people. Been that way since he was a kid. He'd get so mad when he'd call one of his friends to play basketball or something and couldn't reach them. He'd call them all day. I'd have to tell him, baby, can't nobody sit around and wait for your call. It meant something for him to be able to reach you when he called. For him to find you if he was looking. He called me and I didn't answer because I turned my phone off. I don't even have a personalized greeting. He couldn't even hear his own mama's voice one last time.

She is becoming emotional. **Spicer** *consoles her.*

Spicer   Baby don't do this. You weren't ignoring him. You were ignoring me. I saw the number pop up on my phone. I saw it. I thought it was you calling me from somebody's phone to fuck with me. So I ignored it. I ain't know. You ain't know. How could we? That our baby boy was calling from some phone he picked up out a puddle of blood. Lord God . . .

And now he shows hurt.

Dr. Ross   We can take a break. We should. Let's break.

Spicer   Nah, I don't want no break. Just rip it off. Let's get it done with.

Dr. Ross   Let me ask you, Spicer, do you believe talking to Gordon that morning would've changed anything now?

Spicer   I wasn't going to be able to transport through the phone and take a bullet for him if that's what you mean.

Dr. Ross   Of course not. But emotionally, mentally . . . do you think you would feel differently?

Spicer   Don't no man want to see his boy come and go. A son is supposed to bury his father. But if it has to be the other way around, then I want to be there with him. I want to . . .

He begins to crack.

I don't want to get no call from someone else telling me something like that about my boy. You understand? I gotta hear it second hand like I ain't his father. Why would I want someone to tell me something about my own son? I brought him into the world but don't see him off? He was calling me, looking for a send-off and I just sat there looking at the phone ring. You damn right it would be different otherwise.

Dr. Ross   It sounds like, to me, you feel as though you let your son down. Is that safe to say?

Spicer/Norma   . . .

Dr. Ross   Perhaps you feel as though you let him down and now there's the situation with your grandbabies. Maybe that has led you to believe your son somehow felt you let him down in ways you never knew.

Spicer/Norma   . . .

Dr. Ross   Spicer?

Spicer, *almost in a daze, suddenly comes back.*

Spicer   I'm here.

Dr. Ross   Perhaps you want to have that last moment as some sort of evidence that you were in fact there for your son when you needed to be. Without it, though, maybe you feel convicted.

Spicer   You telling me or you asking me? Huh? Sound like you telling me. That's what we're paying you for? For you to tell *us* how *we* feel? I thought you ask questions and we give answers. You do questions. We do answers! But we done flipped that I see. Alright, so I'll ask the questions then. Let me start with what the hell do you know about me or my son? You know he dead and you know I'm hurting.

Norma   / Spicer, settle down.

Spicer   You spend God knows how much on your schooling which ultimately taught you a dead man's father will grieve. Fucking kudos to you, doc. You're some type of goddamn genius, aren't you?

Norma   Spicer!

Dr. Ross   No, it's okay. Please, Spicer, continue.

Spicer   I ain't gonna feel guilty about something I didn't know I did. My son had every right to make the choice he made. He's a man. Them his kids. But if I did something to make him go that way, I never knew. I ain't gonna feel guilty about the unknown. If I step on your shoes and scuff 'em up, I'll get down on my knees to wipe 'em off. I'll make it right. But you wanna walk ten miles down the road after the fact and tell the world Spicer Jones stepped on your shoes and made 'em dirty. You tell everyone else but me and I'm supposed to . . . what? Feel guilty? I didn't even know I stepped on 'em, motherfucker!

Dr. Ross   So, the fact your son and his wife named Kiko as the guardian of his kids doesn't bother you?

Spicer   I didn't say that. I said I don't feel guilty.

Dr. Ross   What do you feel?

Spicer   MAD! CONFUSED! Shit. I'm pissed off. I cut you that bad, huh? Where was the blood? Where were the tears? Why ain't you tell me? Like a man! Instead of hiding behind some sorry ass last will and testament.

Gordon *emerges again.* **Spicer** *receives him.* **Gordon** *is in college.*

Gordon   What's going on, Pops?

Spicer   Hey, boy, you ain't got no track meet this week?

Gordon   Yeah we do but I did something to my knee. I'm taking a week off before the conference championship.

Spicer   I see. So, what you doing here in the middle of the week? Shouldn't you be studying for finals or something at least?

Gordon   I think you know why I'm here, Pops.

Spicer   Yeah, yeah. I figured. So what your mama tell you this time?

Gordon   She told me you put your hands on her . . . again. (*Beat.*) I thought we were past all that shit, man?

Spicer   And what she say she did? Huh? Or I'm just the villain every single time?

Gordon   Nah she told me the whole story. And I'm going to talk to her too but what you want me to do, Pops? That's my mama and she tells me a man put his hands on her. If it was somebody else out there in the world I'm supposed to go beat they ass or give it my best shot.

Spicer   So what you saying, boy? You sure you wanna ride that ride? You ready?

Gordon   I don't want to do a lot of things. I don't want to take this physics exam next week. Not sure I'm ready for that either. But I gotta do it. And we gonna see what happens.

Spicer   Listen, Gordon, you . . . you just don't know. You're gonna know, but you don't know yet. The world can get you to believe you're things you didn't think you could be. Behave in ways you didn't think you could. But your world ain't been that ugly yet. So ugly that it rubs off on you. And I pray it never is, but experience tells me you'll be up against it at some time or another. And you'll have to decide what you're going to do. Who you're gonna be. And that's where I'm at, I gotta make a decision and I'm gonna make the right one, son. I am. I'm gonna make this right.

Gordon   You been saying that, Pops.

Spicer   Well, I ain't dead am I? I still got time. Shit. (*Beat.*) I know you don't like all this shit that goes on between me and your mama. And you shouldn't. It ain't fair. But life ain't fair. It's just the way it is—God is real and the world is cold. All we can do is keep trying.

Gordon   You ain't gotta tell me about life. I know how life works. I know how the world works too. You ain't the only one with a story.

Spicer   Oh you got stories now?

Gordon   I got plenty. I know they can't ever possibly measure up to yours though. My life ain't shit compared to yours. You've seen it all, done it all, and been it all. All there ever was to / see or be.

Spicer   You goddamn right I have! Everything but a punk and a bitch. I been a poor woman's dream and a rich woman's pet. I've been God's champion and I been his biggest disappointment. I've been on both ends of the food chain—the hunter and the prey. And maybe I had to go down that path to learn enough to keep you from doing the same. To give you all I've given you. Now, you want to stand in my face with your chest all puffed out and your fist cocked, looking like you want your ass whooped. Implying you seen something I ain't or that you know something I don't. But, boy, you don't know shit! You hear me?! YOU DON'T KNOW A MOTHERFUCKING THING!

Gordon   . . . I know you better not ever put your hands on my mother again.

He says this boldly but nervously. Not out of fear, but he loves his old man. Respects the hell out of him. He's trying to prove himself. Not hurt **Spicer** *and* **Spicer** *gets this. But it still hurts. And* **Spicer** *hurt looks like* **Spicer** *angry. He stares at his son then moves away, back to the couch.* **Norma** *approaches her son.*

Norma   You heading off?

Gordon   Yeah. I need to get back to school.

Norma   Hey . . . what did you say to your father? I didn't tell you those things for you to confront him. I don't want to drive a wedge between you two.

Gordon   You don't? You don't want me to pick sides? Pick your side? Then what you tell me for? (*Beat.*) And matter fact, why is he catching you on the phone with that nigga?

Norma   Watch your mouth. He didn't *catch* me doing anything. I wasn't being sneaky. Gary called me out of the blue. And maybe I should've hung up on him but I didn't. It was harmless. Your father walked in and I told him exactly who it was. The man was just catching up. Talking about his kids.

Gordon   Did you talk about yours? Because that motherfucker don't need to know shit about me.

Norma   Hey now!

Gordon   Oh I'm sorry, *Uncle Gary* doesn't need to know anything about me. (*Beat.*) Can't believe this fool is calling people up. Disrupting shit. I pray every night I randomly see him one day. In a store. In the street. In a church. I'll beat his ass in the name of God. Watch me!

Norma   Who you think you're talking to?!

Gordon   You was supposed to be staying at Aunt Kim's. I was supposed to be visiting you there. Instead you got me at this nigga's house walking around in my tighty-whities, he's lounging around, you skipping around in a robe like we're a family. Like he's my daddy. You got over on me when I was nine, Mama, but I'm twenty-one now and I've got questions. Why the hell is he calling all this time later? How you expect Pops to react?

Norma   Who you think you are? Questioning me! What I did was wrong. And I paid for it. Over and over again. Trust me, that debt was never forgiven. It was paid! In full! Plus interest! I told you the man called me out the blue. I told your daddy too. And now I'm done with it. Me and your daddy has moved on. I shouldn't have told you nothing. Just forget it.

Gordon   What you mean y'all done moved on?

Norma   Me and your daddy is alright now. We talked. We got an understanding.

Gordon   What kind of understanding? I come home two days ago and your bags are packed. Now you all understand each other?

Norma   See, you wanna say you're grown but you acting like a kid all over again. You and your sister never liked to see me and your father reconcile. Never. You two thought we needed your permission. But we didn't need it then and we don't need it now. Parents argue. They fight. They make mistakes. They move on.

Gordon   You two are unstable, Mama. You know that? And you wonder why sis took a job a thousand miles away the second she got a chance. Why she don't ever come back home. What you think is normal ain't normal, Mama. (*Beat.*) Don't ever ... and I mean ever ... call me with this mess again. It ain't right.

He leaves. **Norma** *stands there.*

Norma   He told us. Not with tears and not with blood. But he told us . . . we cut him. We just didn't listen.

Scene Three

Kiko *sits in the office across from* **Dr. Ross**. *He seems nervous.*

Dr. Ross   Thank you for being here, Kiko.

Kiko   Not a problem.

Dr. Ross   You nervous?

Kiko   I don't know. Maybe a little. I haven't done this before. You know—therapy. Seeing a shrink. I'm waiting to see what you're gonna ask.

Dr. Ross   Well, what we're doing here is somewhat different. The therapy isn't for you necessarily so don't feel as though you're under a microscope. Just . . . talk to me. Then we'll bring in Gordon's parents and you can talk to them. I appreciate you being here and being willing to open up. It means a lot to Spicer and Norma as well.

Kiko   Yeah, well, I'd do anything for Mr. and Mrs. Jones. But they didn't have to bring me here to get me to do it. To talk to them or tell them whatever they want to know.

Dr. Ross   They're having a hard time knowing what to say. Or what to ask.

Kiko   I get it.

Dr. Ross   So, you've known them a long time?

Kiko   Yeah. Pretty much my whole life. Met Gordon in kindergarten and the rest was history.

Dr. Ross   Were you surprised that Gordon and Erica left their kids to you?

Kiko   Yeah, surprised. But not confused.

Dr. Ross   Elaborate, please.

Kiko   I don't know. I don't really want to say some shit that seems like I'm disparaging Mr. and Mrs. Jones. They're good parents. Good people. Great grandparents.

Dr. Ross   I understand. However, what you say to me will stay between us. What you choose to share with them is completely up to you. But whereas you aren't confused by Gordon's decision, they are. Any light you can shed could be helpful.

Kiko   Gordon lived seven houses down from me. Same block. Same hood. We didn't live in the *gutter* by any means but there were some folks going through it. Wasn't shit to see some folks outside all hours of the night cause their lights was off.

So they would use the street lights. Or set the milk out on the porch to keep it cold during the winter. Use the stove for heat. My family was one of them. But you wasn't ever gonna go to Gordon's house and not have lights, something to eat, running water. You know what I'm saying? You flush the toilet and that thing gonna flush a thousand times out of thousand times. Same with flipping the light switch. But, on the other hand, you could go to his house at any time and just as easily find his mama not there. She'd leave two and three months at a time sometimes. Or you could go there and see his daddy tripping. Yelling. Screaming. Fussing. For the whole neighborhood to hear. And who was gonna say something to Spicer Jones? Shit. Not my fifteen-year-old ass. Not even my daddy. Spicer Jones was somebody. And somebody you ain't want to fuck with at certain times. Anyways, I guess this is what I'm getting at. You need food. You need water. You need heat and shit, right? But peace of mind is looked at as a luxury. A non-essential for a kid. But see my household had peace. My old man ain't dare call my mom's out her name and my mama didn't talk to everybody like they were her puppets. Under her control. We had peace. Didn't always have lights. But peace? We had that. Now, I do a pretty good job of keeping the lights on in my own house; I'm grown now. But if I had to part with one, either peace or the lights . . . it's easy. It'd be the lights. Sun gonna come up in the morning. But how you gonna supplement peace? I think that's the kinda place Gordon would rather have his kids at.

Dr. Ross   Thank you. (*Beat.*) Mind if I bring in Spicer and Norma now?

Kiko   Okay.

Dr. Ross *leaves and returns shortly with* **Spicer** *and* **Norma**. *They take a seat.*

Dr. Ross   So, here we are. First off, thank you, each of you, for being here. Now, as I understand you all haven't actually spoken with one another in quite some time.

Norma   Yes. It's been a while. (*Beat.*) Kiko, how are you?

Kiko   I'm doing good, Mrs. Jones. I'd ask you but considering where we're at . . .

Norma   Right.

Dr. Ross   And why is that? Why haven't you all spoken? Spicer, Norma—do you feel any sort of resentment towards Kiko?

Norma   What? No. Of course not.

Kiko *makes a face, perhaps grunts—incredulous.*

Dr. Ross   Kiko, you'd like to add something to that?

Kiko   I guess I just don't understand then. I mean, why haven't you talked to me, Mrs. Jones? I come by to drop the kids off so you could see them and you open the door just enough for them to walk in. Leave me on the porch. I called to ask you your opinion on something. What you think they might like for Christmas, trying to include you, never got a call back. It's been eight months since I've had them and I've seen you three times. Ain't seen you at all, Mr. Jones. Anita drops the kids off though and she gets invited in. You beg her to stay for dinner. I ain't crying about it. I don't want to be anywhere I'm not wanted. I'm just asking what is it? If it's not resentment?

Spicer   It's consideration. That's what it is.

Dr. Ross   Consideration for whom?

Spicer   Kiko! That's who. I don't say much cause I don't want to say the wrong thing. I don't want to judge you. Don't want to make you uncomfortable. You got the kids. You're who Gordon entrusted. But personally, I don't think you're qualified. You the baby of all your siblings. Ain't been close to getting married or settling down. Never had nobody to look after. You got Anita but how long that thing gonna last, Kiko? Hell, all the time I've known you, you done got more women than shit got flies.

Kiko   That ain't who I am anymore, Mr. Jones. I've slowed down since Anita. Just like when Gordon met Erica.

Norma   All due respect, Kiko, but Gordon was never out there like that.

Kiko   Like what?

Norma   I'm not under the impression my son was some virginal saint but come on, Kiko . . . you had girls popping up at our house for God's sake looking for you.

Kiko   . . .

Dr. Ross   Kiko?

Kiko   She's right. That happened once. But what makes you think Gordon was doing something different? That a girl ain't pop up at my folks' house a time or two for him? Because you didn't know about it?

Spicer   My son was focused on school and running track. Then he graduated and that focus moved to his job and then Erica and them kids.

Kiko   All I'm saying is before Erica, I saw him balance school and women, track and women, his job and women, just fine. Whatever it was, there was always women. Then. He. Met. Erica. I'm just saying, I'm focused now too. I have to be. Letting anyone down—the kids, Anita, you all—it isn't an option for me.

Norma   Kiko, you're a good guy. You was a great friend to my son. I'm sure great things are destined for you. We don't question that or your intentions. But Gordon was cut from a different cloth. His ambitions were different.

Kiko   I think you're doing quite a bit of assuming here, Mrs. Jones. I think you want to believe things about your son you never took the time to actually find out.

Norma   Excuse me? No, I think you're doing some assuming now, Kiko.

Dr. Ross   I'd like to let Kiko finish. If that's alright with you, Norma and Spicer. We've asked him here, we should at least listen.

Kiko   I'm just saying me and Gordon weren't that different. So, either you don't know me or you didn't know him.

Spicer   Boy, maybe you ain't know him! Friends grow up. Grow apart. Nah, I ain't know his every move but that don't mean I didn't know him. I knew my son.

Norma   What are you trying to imply? You knew something that we didn't, Kiko? (*To* **Dr. Ross**.) Is that fair? Can I ask that?

Dr. Ross   You can ask whatever you'd like. Whatever Kiko is comfortable answering.

Kiko   I'll answer anything.

Norma   Well, then, what'd you know that we didn't?

Kiko   I know he thought you two were immovable. You didn't bend. You were demanding. Unfair. Judgmental.

Gordon *enters, he's angry. Bubbling over with emotions.* **Kiko** *approaches him.*

Kiko   What the hell is wrong with you?

Gordon   I can't do it no more, man. My folks . . . they won't stop. They can't stop being how they are. Shit ain't ever gonna change.

Kiko   What happened this time?

Gordon   You know my mama was gone for a while.

Kiko   Again?

Gordon   What you mean *again*? It's tradition now. She was gone which means my pops was staying out late every night. Andrea's gone to college, so it's been just me at the crib. Which I don't mind but /

Kiko   You sure? Sounds like you need me to spend the night, nigga. You lonely? We can make smores and shit.

Gordon   I'm serious, man.

Kiko   Alright. So what's going on?

Gordon   My mama suddenly pops back in like nothing happened. I come home after track practice and there she is. Her and my daddy all close and shit.

Norma *and* **Spicer** *approach all giggly and shit.*

Spicer   You gonna make it spicy like I like it?

Norma   Extra spicy, baby.

Spicer   Then I'm gonna need something sweet afterwards.

Norma   That's what you got me for.

Gordon   Uh . . . what's up y'all?

Spicer   Oh hey, boy! You hungry? Your mama's making jambalaya.

Norma   You know he's hungry if I'm making that. Even if he ain't he'll make room. Won't you, baby boy? You gotta make room for some of your mama's jambalaya!

Gordon   Maybe. I'm not too hungry now.

Norma   You're always hungry after track practice.

Gordon   Well . . . I'm not now.

Spicer   What the hell is wrong with you? Why you in such a pissy mood?

Norma   Hmph . . . you know why. Every time I come back he acts like this.
Probably because he knows someone is going to be watching over him a little closer.
He thinks he's grown when ain't nobody here to keep him in check.

Spicer   Hell you know I'm working all the time. I can't be here to monitor his every
move.

Norma   I know, baby. I ain't saying you done anything wrong. But now he can't just
do whatever he wants. And every time I come back this is how he acts.

Gordon   Maybe it shouldn't be a thing where you're always coming back, Mama.
Maybe you shouldn't always be leaving.

Spicer   Whoa now! Who the fuck you think you're talking to? That's my wife. Your
mother! She here and she's here to stay. If you don't like you can get the hell on, boy.
I'll put your ass out over her if it come to that. I don't want it to, but if does, if you're
drawing a line in the sand, I don't want you to be confused on where I stand, you
hardheaded motherfucker. You follow me?

Gordon   Oh, I'm right behind you, Pops. You've made that clear a thousand times
before.

Norma   You know what? Just go on to your room. Selfish, thoughtless little bastard;
I swear. You and your sister do this. Matter fact, cut the grass like you're supposed to.
Clean up your room like you're supposed to. And stay there for the rest of the night
with your little seventeen-year-old ass. Thinking you grown.

Spicer and **Norma** *return to the couch.*

Kiko   Damn, man. They came at you with that bullshit?

Gordon   I'm tired of it, man. I ain't gonna be too many more motherfuckers and
bastards. I ain't gonna keep doing everything I'm supposed to while they do whatever
the fuck they want. You know?

Kiko   I hear you.

Gordon   They get to talk to me however they want because they "Mama and Daddy."
*You better go to school on time and do what you're told, boy! You better do your
homework and get good grades, boy! You better do what we tell you, boy!* All the while
they got the longest leash in the world. They ain't got nobody to answer to and nothing
to answer for let them tell it. I can't take this shit, man. They're squashing me. I wanna
be anywhere but where I'm fucking at. Anywhere . . . even in the fucking ground.

He is showing some emotion. Type of emotion a nigga his age ain't supposed to show.
Kiko *then does something a nigga like him ain't supposed to do. And he hugs his
friend. Tightly. Let him know he's here for him. Ain't afraid to show affection. Nah, it's
a hug. He loves his friend. What a concept, huh? Then they break, shake hands, and*
Gordon *leaves.* **Kiko** *remains standing as he addresses* **Norma** *and* **Spicer**.

Kiko   I know he loved you both. Mr. Jones, I ain't ever seen anyone lift someone so high. You were everything to him. And he adored you too, Mrs. Jones. But there were things he didn't want his kids to see. Things he wasn't sure you could keep away.

Spicer   These things were years ago. Goddamn. A man gotta be perfect now?

Norma   We won't win no parent of the year awards but we did our best. I can say that.

Spicer   Damn sure did.

Dr. Ross   Perhaps Gordon was built to handle what you exposed him to but he didn't want to run the risk with his kids.

Spicer   *Expose? Run the risk?* What does any of that shit mean? Exposed to what? The boy had it good.

Dr. Ross   By what measure?

Spicer   Every damn measure! Kiko you make it seem like we ain't did nothing good for the boy! Like he hated his life. Nah, I didn't do everything right all the time. I got some shit to answer for. Shit I've done to his mama. To him. His sister. I ain't ignorant. And I ain't self-righteous. Hell, I called Earl Jefferson a bitch ass nigga in front of his woman thirty years ago. She told him to light me up for saying it. He wouldn't. So then she called him a bitch ass nigga too and left him. I suppose I'll have to answer for that as well. And I'll answer for it all. When the call comes, I'll pick it up. Yes God, it's me. And I did this and I did that. I did. But how many times did I give a motherfucker my lunch just cause he was hungrier than me? Or a little piece of money even though I didn't have it to give? Sometimes I walked around with the world on my back without a single strap to hold on to. How many times I tell my son never do the things I do, not cause I'm a hypocrite but cause I want him to be a better person. A better man than me! I done some good too. And I resent the implication I haven't. The boy done went and got himself killed and left this to hang over my head. He knew what he was doing. And why? Cause I never came back and said sorry?

He is nearing a rage.

Well, I am. And if he was here I'd get down on my hands and knees. I'd kneel before his feet and kiss them and tell him how motherfucking sorry I am!

A moment. His apologies are becoming more sincere.

I'm sorry you had to see those things between me and your mama. I'm sorry that sometimes your home felt like anything but. I'm sorry I didn't answer your call that day. I'm sure enough one sorry motherfucker. Any man who sends his boy out into the world with gashes and wounds and bruises and lets them harden over is . . . he's sorry. And I'm sorry. But you ain't here no more to hear me say it. But I am . . . I'm sorry, son.

Intermission—if one is scheduled.

Scene Four

A few weeks later. **Dr. Ross** *is with* **Norma**.

Dr. Ross   I take it Spicer won't be joining us this week.

Norma   That's right.

Dr. Ross   As was the case last week.

Norma   Correct.

Dr. Ross   And the week before that.

Norma   This is all correct. Yes.

Dr. Ross   Yet you've come faithfully. It's been somewhat more difficult to get you to talk without him here if I'm being frank. Nonetheless, you're here. Why is that?

Norma   Curiosity, I guess.

Dr. Ross   Regarding?

Norma   My daughter challenged me. First, she accused me. She cast aspersions on me. Things I don't believe are right. Then she dared me to speak with someone and see for myself.

Dr. Ross   You don't speak much about your daughter.

Norma   What's there to say? My son is dead. I've struggled with that but I accepted it long ago. I had to. Oh I called his phone. I went and knocked on his door. Several times. But he didn't answer. I searched in my grandbabies' faces hoping he was somehow reincarnated. And what kind of grandmother does that make me? Still, I didn't see him. I accepted it because otherwise I'm just crazy. But I'm not here to help me move on. I'm here because he saw his father and I as unfit guardians to his children and my daughter has implied the reasoning—which we fail to see—is locked away in a past we don't remember. She said we need help remembering, help she ain't qualified to give. So I'm here. Talking to you. Waiting for you to tell me who is right—me or her. But I don't get how talking about her helps.

Dr. Ross   How did she take losing her brother?

Norma   Well, my daughter is strong, Dr. Ross. Mmm hmm. She's made of something the world has never seen. Her strength offends me if I'm being honest. Not just me. Her father too. I've saw it offend a lot of folks. It comes off as calloused. Or unconcerned. She's not cold. Don't get me wrong. She's warm. She can befriend a rock and the rock will roll beside her forever. I've saw it happen. But long ago she convinced herself that her life was just that—hers. And she's got to live it. For the first time since she was ten I saw her scared. I saw her crack. I saw her confused. When she lost her brother. And what good was I? I was scared, I was cracking, I was confused tenfold.

Dr. Ross   So her and Gordon were close?

Norma   Inseparable. My and her father did that. They can take anything from us but they can't take that. They wouldn't even try. We told them they better pick each other and hang on to each other over anyone else; even us.

Dr. Ross   Was it a surprise that the kids weren't left with her then?

Norma   She says it wasn't.

Andrea *enters with a box used for packing.* **Norma** *approaches her.*

Andrea   I really don't want to talk about this right now, Mama.

Norma   If we don't talk about it now, you'll go back home and won't have time to talk about it ever again. Can't you just talk to me? I've given you space. But I'd like to talk to you. Been waiting for you to come back. I'd thought you'd come back home more often after all this. Been six months and I've saw you once. Now you're here. I'm just asking, if not me and your father why not you? Why? What about family?

Andrea   I'm a mover. I'm on the go. Always. Okay? Yes, I would have moved back and changed my whole life for them kids and he knew that. But in the few conversations we've had, I got the impression he wanted them with someone who saw themselves having kids. Who wanted kids. The kids love Kiko.

Norma   You don't want kids?!

Andrea   I'm closer to forty than I am to thirty. Closer to fifty than twenty. I haven't had a serious relationship since college and you've never heard me complain, cry, or dwell on any of the above. My life is moving forward and I'm moving on day by day without thinking about what I don't have. It's not about if I want kids or not, I'm just okay without them. Or maybe that's semantics. Maybe I don't want them. I don't know.

Norma   So he leaves them with Kiko?

Andrea   Anyone who knows Gordon and Kiko knows if you can't have one the other is the next best thing.

Norma   Kiko isn't Gordon.

Andrea   Right. He's the next best thing.

Norma   Kiko is a womanizing whore.

Andrea   By that same measure then I guess I'm a man-eating hoe.

Norma   Then I guess it's best the kids weren't left with you after all.

Andrea   Wow. You're right. I don't understand at all why Gordon didn't leave his kids with a judgmental, hypocritical, entitled ass woman.

Norma   You better watch your mouth!

Andrea   You watch yours! Gordon was a decent man.

Norma   I know what he was! He was my son!

Andrea   And my brother! You aren't the only one who gets to speak on him. Who gets to know something about him. He was a good husband and great father. Who are you to question decisions he made for his kids?

Norma   Why are you like this? Huh? You lost your brother. I don't know how that feels. I'd run up and hug you if you'd let me. Hug you for however long it took. But I lost my son. You haven't once tried to comfort me. You've been cold, Andrea. And mechanical. On a mission. Come here, help pack up Gordon's things, and go on back home. Have you even called your father to check on him?

Andrea   Has he called me?

Norma   He would if he felt like you wanted him to.

Andrea   Why would he assume I didn't?

Norma   You know your father.

Andrea   That's not fair. What he does or what he doesn't do is excused by the fact he is who he is. But you want to give me a guilt trip? Extend me the same courtesy, Mama. I'm just being me. He's just being him. And like always, you're just being you.

Norma   And what the fuck does that supposed to mean with your grown ass?

Andrea   Yes. Thank you. Very grown indeed. The fact you say it sarcastically, as if I'm not, is strange to me.

Norma   I'm just trying to talk to you.

Andrea   Exactly. You want to talk but you never want to listen.

Norma   Well, I'm listening now! And I'm begging you to tell me something. Anything. (*Beat.*) Me and your father has a wall full of birthday cards and Mother's Day cards and Father's Day cards that you two wrote. Telling us you were happy. You were proud. You were blessed. To come from where you came from. What was that?

Andrea   It was the truth. It stands on its own. There's other truths too, though.

Norma   Like what?

Andrea   I don't know, Mama. Like . . . the clay doesn't get mad at the fire for being so hot. Because now it's a vase and its functional and sturdy and beautiful and valuable. But maybe sometimes the clay wonders if it was even supposed to be a vase. Or if the fire was needed. Maybe it was supposed to be mortar. Or a dam. Or the cream you put on your face to take away the wrinkles. I don't know . . . maybe there was just another way.

Norma   Sounds like you're saying you and your brother didn't need us. That you'd be better without us. Further along.

Andrea   You're hearing what you want to hear, Mama. To justify feeling wronged. So you can then be mad at Gordon. Because being mad at him helps take away the pain. But you asked for a truth. For some light and I'm trying to give that to you.

Norma   So that's how Gordon felt?

Andrea   I don't know. I'm telling you how I feel. That's the only thing I know with absolute certainty. Gordon had a wife to confide in. To vent to. Hell, I got questions too, Mama. But he's not here for me to ask him. I'm just telling you how I feel and maybe some sense can be made of other things. (*Beat.*) Never once . . . and I mean not one damn time have I or Gordon ever talked about where we could be or who we'd be without you and daddy. We needed you. But it was heavy sometimes, Mama. So . . . fucking heavy. So hot. It was hell. And maybe you didn't have to be fire. Maybe you two could've been water. Or wind. Or the heat from the sun to mold us how you saw fit. Do you understand what I'm saying?

Norma   No. I really don't, Andrea. I don't have a goddamn clue right now. Water, wind, and the sun my ass. If I had to try and call it, it sounds like you're saying we did everything wrong and somehow, by the grace of God, you and your brother turned out alright. Despite me and your father's best efforts to turn you around and get you all mixed up.

Andrea   See . . . that's why no one talks to you. You say whatever you want and hear whatever you want. I'm asking you to look back and try to understand why things are the way they are now and if you might have had anything at all to do with it. Instead of playing the victim.

Norma   I pray to God when you have kids, *if* you have kids, they don't persecute you for every single mistake you / ever—

Andrea   Come on, Mama! Don't do that. No one is attacking you. I'm asking you to take accountability.

Norma   No, you're asking me to take nothing but blame and no credit. I didn't fail you or your brother.

Andrea   I didn't say / you did.

Norma   You and your father and your brother huddled up and had your inside jokes at my expense. Because I wasn't vulgar you called me self-righteous. Because I didn't want to be your friend but wanted to be your mother—that made me controlling! But oh, I was there kissing boo boos all along the way wasn't I? Up throughout the middle of the night rubbing you down with Vicks. And I stayed on those teachers' asses if they got out of line. I always took you and your brother's back. Always! Baking cakes. Getting you everything on your Christmas list. Then I came in handy, didn't I? Cooking two and three different dinners. Trying to please everybody. I did the best I could. If that's cliché. If that's me making excuses or dodging accountability, then that's just what it is.

Andrea   That's right, Mama. You did all that and more. And that's why you got that wall full of handwritten cards for your birthday and Mother's Day. But now try and see the other side of it. You see the good you did and what it got you. Now see the other side. Are you looking? Can you see it?

Norma   I'm trying to.

Andrea   Maybe you and Daddy need to talk to somebody. To help you see it. Cause I can't help you, Mama. You lost your son. I lost my brother. You want to know why he left his kids with Kiko. I still want to know why he had to be at that fucking factory, why that was the day he had to drop Erica off, when that psychotic motherfucker went in there and killed a bunch of folks including my brother! That's what I want to know. That's what I'm dealing with.

She leaves. **Norma** *remains. Filled with emotion.* **Dr. Ross** *stands and approaches her.*

Dr. Ross   Are you okay?

Norma   You have any kids?

Dr. Ross   Two. A son and a daughter. Just like you.

Norma   Both of them alive and well?

Dr. Ross   Umm . . . yes. (*Beat.*) But let's keep talking about this though. We're making strides. Were you able to process any of what your daughter said?

Norma   What does that mean?

Dr. Ross   Well, by processing it I mean that / you—

Norma   No, I asked if they were alive and well and there was . . . hesitation.

Dr. Ross   I'd really like to focus on you and some of the things your daughter said.

Norma   . . .

Dr. Ross   Alright. My daughter is doing well. I see her often. Every week for dinner. My son not so much.

Norma   Fractured relationship?

Dr. Ross   My son has made some questionable decisions in life. Some of which have led him to move around a lot. Evade. Run. Dodge.

Norma   The law?

Dr. Ross   Yes, that too.

Norma   I find that hard to believe.

Dr. Ross   Our children aren't solely products of what we give them or show them. Some of who they are is just them.

Norma   So, no blame to be had on your end? Because I see it the same. You do your best, they get grown and they have to figure out how to win with the hand they were dealt.

Dr. Ross   Well, I blame myself sometimes.

Norma   But why? If you did your best.

Dr. Ross   I think our best is a very relative thing depending on whatever we're supposedly doing our best at in that moment. It's certainly possible to be the best in one area and miss the mark on others. I fed my son my best. I hugged him my best. I encouraged him my best. But did I explain things the best I could have? Did I listen to him the best I could have?

Norma   So, you have regrets? Which by all accounts, are pretty useless. No?

Dr. Ross   I'm confident my husband and I gave my son the tools to choose right from wrong, good from bad, what's best and not best . . . for him. Do I wish he made a different decision? Absolutely. But more than that I wish for him peace, so he can live with his decision. I trust what I put into him. Now, was some of what I put into him too much militancy? Extremism? Is he too individualistic? I've asked myself that. Sure. But at the end of the day he made decisions. Just like your son made a decision. It wasn't to hurt you. It wasn't out of spite. You have to trust if nothing else he thought it was simply the right thing to do. Sometimes doing the right thing costs you. Just like the wrong thing. So, it's hard to tell which is which. You just have to know. In this instance your son doing what he felt was right came at the expense of you and your husband's feelings. That had to have been hard for him. Don't feel like you don't know your son though. Don't feel like the good you remember is just a mirage. Just be open to learning something new. It can't be easy to know your kids never healed from certain things or that there were even things to heal from. But what's even harder is as that kid, attempting to heal from something all the while acting like it never happened. Gordon and Andrea were left to process a lot of things on their own. I'd challenge you, much like your daughter, to at least see where your son was coming from. To see it . . . then acknowledge it.

Scene Five

Norma *and* **Spicer** *stand close to one another. A flashback.*

Spicer   I'm not signing this shit. This is crazy. And you know it is.

Norma   What do you suggest then?

Spicer   I suggest we honor a vow. One we took before God. One we ain't thought about breaking all this time. I don't want to even entertain this shit. Tell me what you need me to do, baby. Tell me. I'll do it. Counseling? Fine. Sleep on the couch? Bad back and all just give me a blanket. But I'm not doing this.

Norma   We've hurt each other every way possible. I'm coming and going as I please. You're just flat out mean now, Spicer. You still heavy handed. Literally and figuratively. Look at my face. And the kids see everything.

Spicer   Is that what it's about then? The kids? Because I told you a long time ago if you wanted to leave then leave. If you wanted to stay gone then stay. But you came back. Because of the kids. Now you want to leave again because of them. Because you think it's best. But I *think* too. You ain't gonna ask me about that?

Norma   Well, then, what do you think, Spicer? Tell me.

Spicer   I think my son been two doors down from his father his whole life. And I don't want to change that. He should find me if he's looking. Every time. Me and Andrea, we don't see eye to eye. She look at me funny. I know that. But I love my baby girl. And I'd like to show her I can do better but I can't do it at a distance. I think you tired of me making the same ol' mistakes and you're right for feeling that way. I need to change. And I will. But us signing this paper means we can't change. You can't stop walking out on me. You can't stop running to some other man. And I don't believe that. We can both stand here and justify and rationalize why we've done things we've done. You run out on me cause I hit you or the way I talk to you. I hit you and talk to you how I do cause you run out on me. But what came first—the chicken or the egg?

Norma   But one of those things certainly came first, Spicer.

Spicer   All I'm saying is let's stop justifying. Let's stop rationalizing. And let's just stop doing the things we're doing, baby. But if you leave me that paper and walk out, then I sign it, don't come back when you find things hurt far more out there than they do here. Cause I can't keep going back and forth.

A moment. She reconsiders.

Norma   We have to change.

Spicer   And we will.

Norma   No, Spicer. We have to. (*Beat.*) You got Gordon. He ain't gonna ever change his mind when it comes to you. You can go out there and rob a bank or kidnap some damn body and he'll figure you did it for the greater good. You and Andrea may not get along but she sure respects the hell out of you. But I'm the weak one. The dependent one. The one who comes back and messes up the flow. Us changing means more for me than it does for you.

Spicer   That's not true. You keep us together. You keep us working. You don't think those kids see that? (*Beat.*) Hell, Andrea looks at me with disgust anytime I open my mouth. I'm qualified to talk about money and nothing else. I can't even give her advice when she goes out on these dates. How can I? When the worst things about men she's already seen, she seen in me. Her father. But we ain't perfect. Nobody is. They understand that.

She's coming around.

Norma   And they know we love them.

Spicer   Damn right they do. The hugs and kisses.

Norma   The presents just because.

Spicer   Just bought the boy a car. Tenth grade and he the only one out of all his friends with the ability to come and go.

Norma   Gave Andrea my car when she left for college. She been asking for it. I barely drove it. Bet nobody at her school got a car that nice.

Spicer   Hell, she called me saying her dorm was too small. Said it smelled funny. Didn't like sharing a shower. I got her a nice apartment down the street.

Norma   We spoil them.

Spicer   Hell yeah we do! And they know it. They got it good. Yeah we made mistakes. But it ain't that bad.

Norma   You don't think so?

Spicer   Hell nah! Love and affection is a helluva equalizer.

Norma   Shit, we're doing a lot better than our parents.

Spicer   A lot damn better.

Norma   Can't be doing too bad. Honor roll students. Haven't gotten into any trouble.

Spicer   No drugs. No pregnancies. No arrests. If they want to blame us for something, blame us for that.

Norma   That's right. We did that. They got structure.

Spicer   What we're supposed to do as parents we do. I'm not talking about a roof or clothes no food. I don't want no parade for that. I'm talking about they got support. They got encouragement. Freedom to dream and go after the world. We gotta have some freedom too though.

Norma   To make mistakes and learn from them. You're never too old for that.

Spicer   Never.

Norma   To do things that make us happy.

Spicer   And you make me happy, baby. More than anything else in this world. You hear me?

Norma   I hear you.

Spicer   And I can change. I can. You believe that, don't you?

Norma   I do. And so can I.

Spicer   I ain't got no doubts.

An embrace and as they embrace **Gordon** *and* **Andrea** *enter.* **Dr. Ross** *continues to look on. The parents continue to embrace while the children speak.*

Gordon   So, what you think?

Andrea   I don't think nothing. You knew what was going to happen.

Gordon   Yeah but I was hoping for a new delivery at least.

Andrea   What, an apology?

Gordon   Hell nah, I knew that wasn't coming. Just something new; shit, entertain me! Instead I walked in right after practice and Mama is in the bed laying on Pop's chest. They're eating popcorn and watching movies. She's feeding him kernel after kernel.

Andrea   I hate and I mean I fucking hate that lovey-dovey shit, man! They be so far up each other's ass once they reunite. They just want to show off. Get on my damn nerves.

Gordon   And Mama was talking about divorce this time. Divorce, my ass!

Andrea   She said she had the papers ready.

Gordon   Showed me a house she was gonna buy.

They both get a good laugh at this.

Andrea   Bless her heart. So, did they even say anything to you when you walked in?

Gordon   Not really. I walked in and Mama said *oh hey, baby*, like she ain't been gone for three months. And they kept eating popcorn.

Andrea   See, that's the shit I can't stand. Mama called me crying. Saying she needed to stay somewhere and might need to stay with me. She's going to fly a thousand miles to me to stay for a week? Yeah okay. I said sure, Mama. Come on down. Please do. I'd love to have you. But see that's not what she wanted me to say. She wanted me to say *oh my God, Mama, what's wrong*? As in what could be so wrong that you would need to fly so far away and stay with me. But I just don't give a shit. I know ain't nothing that wrong. So I didn't even give her an opening. I just said let me know when you get here.

Gordon   And what she say?

Andrea   She said thanks and then apologized for the inconvenience. But not a real apology.

Gordon   Of course not. Let me guess, she gave you the ol' say-sorry-a-hundred-times-and-ain't-nan-one-of-them-sincere routine. *I'm so sorry Andrea. I'm sorry, I'm sorry, I'm sorry. I know I'm a bother. I know the last thing you want in this world is your mother staying with you. I know I'm a burden. I'm sorry. I'll try and stay out your way. Woe is me.*

Andrea   Exactly. Whoa is her more than whoa been any-damn-body! She put on a show just to get her happy ass back in bed eating popcorn.

Gordon   Kernels was falling all on Pops' chest and shit. He was just straight up glistening. Ol' buttery ass chest and she just eating them right out his chest hairs.

Andrea   Godammit! Okay, that's enough imagery.

Gordon   Got hair all in her teeth.

Andrea (*screams*)   Fuck, man!

Gordon   My bad. (*Beat.*) So how long before you go back to school?

Andrea   I'm leaving the day after tomorrow. You ready to graduate?

Gordon   Hell yeah. High school down. College next.

Andrea   You'll love college.

Gordon   I don't love no kind of school. (*Beat.*) Hey, how long you think before they get into it again?

Andrea   It depends if you mean getting into it in a big way or little way. If we're talking a little way, they're probably arguing now. Probably because Mama left some butter on his chest and that somehow led to him being late somewhere. *I had to take a long ass shower cause you left all that butter in my chest hairs.*

Gordon   Oh so you wanna get me started on that?

Andrea   No! Please! I take it back. (*Beat.*) Anyways, I give 'em a week.

Gordon *acknowledges this with a nod. Then they turn to their parents who break out of their embrace and go straight into war.*

Spicer   Fuck you, Norma! You hear me? Fuck you and I mean it!

Norma   And fuck you! Always think you're right about something. I shouldn't have come back. I should've stayed gone. The kids are grown. Andrea is anyways. Gordon is right behind her. And I let you convince me to stay for them. I'm a fool.

Spicer   I ain't convince you of shit! You ol' lying ass, crazy ass woman! I told you if you go then stay gone this time, damn it. I said I want my boy two doors down from me where he always been and that's the way it's gonna be until he graduates. As for Andrea, well she gonna take your side no matter what. She'll see the truth eventually.

Norma   And what's the truth? Huh? Cause you're just the most upstanding, truthful son of a bitch there ever was. Please tell me what the truth is.

Spicer   I'm more truthful than you. Why don't you just go on back out there to your man Gary.

Norma   I might.

Spicer   And I'll run his ass off a motherfucking cliff. Watch and see.

Norma   Gary can handle his own.

Spicer   You better hope he can. Keep on, Norma. Keep on using that big mouth.

Norma   Kiss my ass, Spicer Jones! Get on your damn knees and kiss my ass—

Spicer *rushes her and raises his hand to her. But he freezes. Everyone freezes but* **Dr. Ross***. She gets up and inspects everyone and everything. Such an ugly situation. She lets out a huge sigh. Then* **Spicer** *leaves and so do the kids. Only* **Norma** *remains, who is no longer still.*

Norma   We aren't proud. There was some shame regarding our behavior. Quite a bit of shame. Paranoia even. God only knows who all knew the inner workings of our marriage. If we were going to explain ourselves to the kids, we probably should've went right down the list. My family. Spicer's family. My friends. His friends. The kids' friends. Kiko. Anita. The grandbabies. It was easier to just try and change and move on.

Dr. Ross   You feel judged?

Norma   That's an understatement if there ever was one.

Dr. Ross   And you think Kiko and Anita are in on it? The perceived judgment?

And then **Anita** *enters. She approaches* **Norma** *while* **Dr. Ross** *goes back to her chair.*

Anita   You guys have a good time? I know you did. They always talk about how much fun they have over here.

Norma (*passive*)   Isn't that nice of them.

Anita   You should come over Tuesday. We're having a little family game night. My sister and her kids are coming over. You and Mr. Spicer should come.

Norma   No, I think we'll pass. Thank you though.

Anita   You sure? You'll have a lot of fun. Come on! What games do you like? I'll pick them up.

Norma   No, really, I'm alright.

Anita   Alright. I just thought /

Norma   Hey, would you like to stay for dinner? I'm sure the kids want to find a way to spend a little more time over here.

Anita   Umm actually we need to head out. Kiko has something planned for us for dinner.

Norma   Oh. Alright then. I guess I'll have them grab their bags and tell them it's time to go.

She steps away and yells for the kids.

Kids! Anita is here! Get your things. Time to go!

Anita   Hey, Ms. Norma, you know anytime you want to come over to see them or you want me to drop them off just let me know.

Norma   Yes, I'll do that.

Anita   Because you can see them anytime. Me and Kiko are fine with it.

Norma   You and Kiko, huh? You know, sweetheart . . . *dear* . . . when you give someone permission to do something they assumed they could do it's a little condescending. It's a real power move to tell the truth.

Anita   I didn't mean it that way.

Norma   . . . How old are you? Wait, don't tell me. My son and Kiko are the same age. You're what? Ten years younger?

Anita   Not quite.

Norma   Not quite that old or not quite that young?

Anita   Not quite that young.

Norma   I see. But you're ready to raise kids? To play Mama to my grandbabies?

Anita   I'm not playing *Mama*. I'm just doing whatever I need to help Kiko.

Norma   So you don't give a damn about the kids: It's just Kiko? You're helping him?

Anita   No, ma'am, that's not what I meant. I'm not trying to be their mother is all I'm saying. However, I am trying to do whatever is needed so they can be happy and healthy . . . I don't know. I just want to be there for them and Kiko.

Norma   Like cooking dinner or washing clothes or picking them up from school or tucking them in?

Anita   That and also things that don't require me wearing an apron.

Norma   Mmm hmm, cute. So in other words, you want to do all the stuff mamas do, yet you're afraid to accept the role of a mama. Too big of a commitment? Not sure you and Kiko can make it?

Anita   No, it's not that.

Norma   Then why aren't you two married?

Anita   We've talked about it. I believe it's the next step for us.

Norma   I see. Well, living together, raising kids together but not being married just isn't something me or Mr. Jones ever believed in. I guess times have changed. Let me ask, do you and Kiko take the kids to church?

Anita   Sometimes.

Norma   Read the Bible to them? Kiko never struck me as a very religious guy.

Anita   Well, neither one of us are well-versed in the Bible to tell the truth. But then again, we don't believe everything in the Bible. It's . . . just a tool.

Norma   A *tool*?! Come again, young lady?

Anita   We know certain parts of the Bible. There's one in the house. We just don't hit the kids over the head with it. Gordon didn't either.

Norma   My son believed in God!

Anita   I know. He just didn't believe everything in the Bible. Erica, him, me, and Kiko talked about these things all the time.

Norma   This is news to me. And truthfully, I find it a little hard to believe.

Anita   You're free to teach them anything you'd like about the Bible, Ms. Norma.

Norma (*emphatic*)   *Mrs. Jones.*

Anita   Okay, I apologize—*Mrs. Jones.*

Norma   And thank you for your permission yet again. I'm glad I can teach *my* grandbabies about the Bible.

A moment.

Anita   I'm sorry . . . I don't . . . have I done something wrong?

Norma *starts to feel bad about how she's behaved.*

Norma   No. No you haven't. But I know what you see when you look at me, Anita. You're Kiko's woman and he's told you everything there is to tell you. Gordon has probably told him everything there was to tell. So you probably know it all. How bad things got between me and Mr. Jones at times. You see me struggling to let my grandbabies go every time you come to pick them up and you laugh to yourself. How dare I question your qualifications, right?

Anita   I don't think that at all.

Norma   Sure you do. And it's okay. Cause, honey, things were ugly between me and my husband at times. Hideous even. Our marriage was like a creature floating thirty thousand feet deep into the ocean. Without eyes and ears, no feelings; just surrounded by nothingness. Only a jagged mouth to feed itself. Oh baby it was bad. But we made it. And our kids turned out alright. I just hope you keep that in mind. You and Kiko.

Anita *gathers her thoughts.*

Anita   When Kiko found out Gordon wanted him to look after the kids we talked the whole night. He talked about what he needed to cut back on. How much money he needed to start saving. Changes that needed to be made. Either renovating his house or buying a new one. He was nervous. He was scared. He was all over the place really. But he was never hesitant to do what Gordon and Erica asked him to do. There wasn't a single doubt that he was going to do it and do it right. And I never asked myself if I wanted to stay and help, I only asked if he wanted me to be there. Everyone is where they want to be Mrs. Jones, except you and Mr. Jones, and I think that's because you feel like you're somehow on the outside, asking to be let in. Having to explain yourselves for something. But you don't have to explain anything to Kiko. Definitely not me. And you're not on the outside. Maybe you should talk to Kiko. Give him a chance. He could really use your help. He told me himself, he needs it. He needs you and Mr. Jones.

She leaves. **Norma** *returns to the couch.*

Dr. Ross   But that wasn't good enough?

Norma   Good enough for what? They were just words. She's a kid trying to say whatever she thinks will make me feel better. She's sweet. Well-intentioned. But the fact remains, we are without our grandbabies.

Dr. Ross   You're not without them. You're just not with them all the time.

Norma   Semantics, Dr. Ross. That's just semantics.

Scene Six

Anita *and* **Andrea** *sit on the couch.* **Kiko** *is standing and paces a bit.* **Dr. Ross** *is in the chair.*

Andrea   And my mother *and* father are coming, right?

Dr. Ross   Yes, that's the plan.

Andrea   Well, this should be something.

Dr. Ross   Can I get you a water or anything, Andrea?

Andrea   No, thank you.

Anita   I have some peppermints.

Andrea   Why? Why would I want that?

Anita   I don't know. Sorry. My mother always kept some and would eat them if she got anxious.

Andrea   I'm not anxious.

Dr. Ross   Or nervous.

Andrea   Certainly not nervous. I know how this is going to go. Still, I'm intrigued. You all got Spicer Jones coming in here for an intervention! This is *grand*! Oh I can't wait.

Kiko   How long are you in town?

Andrea   Leaving tomorrow morning.

Kiko   Never in town long.

Andrea   Long is a subjective term, my brother.

Office phone rings. **Dr. Ross** *answers.*

Dr. Ross   Yes. Please send them in. (*To* **Andrea**.) They're here.

A moment passes and **Spicer** *and* **Norma** *enter*

Spicer   Oh, come the hell on. What is this shit?

Andrea   Hey, Daddy. Hey, Mama.

Spicer   Baby girl? You come in town and don't stop by to see me and your mother?

Andrea   I knew I'd see you here.

She hugs her folks.

Dr. Ross   Thanks for coming, Spicer. It's been a while.

Spicer   Yeah, yeah, yeah. (*To* **Norma**.) What is this about?

Norma   I'm not exactly sure myself. Dr. Ross asked me to come and bring you. (*Beat.*) Well, we're here.

Dr. Ross   Yes, please, take a seat.

Kiko   Mr. Jones, how are you doing, sir?

Spicer   I'm doing alright, young man. You?

Kiko   No complaints.

Spicer   So, what are we doing? A séance? We gonna bring Gordon back?

Dr. Ross   No, not quite. We are, however, going to do our best to channel him in a way.

Spicer   Well, I don't get into all that shit. I let the dead rest.

Norma   What do you mean exactly, Dr. Ross?

Dr. Ross   If you remember, a couple months ago, I left you with a few questions to ask one another. One of which was what was the last thing you said to your son. Today I want to pose a different question. And I believe I know what your answer will be. If I'm correct, then having Kiko and Andrea here will prove very useful. (*Beat.*) Before we start, can I get you guys anything?

Spicer   / No.

Norma   I'm fine. Thank you.

Dr. Ross   Alright, so my question is, and take your time answering if needed, we know the last thing you said to your son, but knowing everything that happened, what would you say to him now if you had one last thing to say?

Spicer/Norma   . . .

Dr. Ross   Here, let's try this, Andrea, what would you say?

Andrea   I left everything on the table with my brother. He was my hero and I was his. He knew that. I'd just say *I love you.*

Dr. Ross   Kiko?

Kiko   I'd just try to make him laugh one good time. Probably tell him the only reason he was faster than me and always beat me on the track was cause my dick was bigger or something and it was harder to maneuver around it. I don't know. Something inappropriate. But I'd just try and make him laugh.

Dr. Ross   Anita, you got to know him well the last couple of years. What about you?

Anita   I guess that I just love him and I'll miss him. That he always made me feel welcomed. Just . . . yeah, all of that.

Dr. Ross   Norma? Spicer?

Norma   I'd just ask him *why.*

Dr. Ross   Specificity matters, Norma.

Norma   I mean, I guess I just /

Spicer   Why the hell did he take our grandbabies from us? Why he do what he did? Why he act like we ain't worthy to look over his kids? Why you ain't want them to have what you had? Why you act like we ain't change none? Like we were monsters or some shit. And why you ain't tell us? Why goddammit? That answer your question?

Dr. Ross   Thank you, Spicer. Yes, it does. That being said, I assumed correctly what both of you would say to your son if he were here. What you would ask him. And while Gordon isn't here, Kiko and Andrea are the ones he would've talked to about those things that led him to make his decision. I tasked them with doing their best to recall any and every conversation pertaining to his kids—what he wanted for them, the father he wanted to be, the mother Erica wanted to be in comparison to what he might have had growing up. They've thought long and hard and both provided very good feedback and came up with a specific, insightful answer that does in fact channel Gordon's own voice. It's the closest we can get if nothing else.

Spicer   In other words, what Andrea and Kiko thinks. Not my boy. No offense, baby girl, but you ain't Gordon. You ain't him.

Andrea   But we talked, Daddy.

Spicer   I talked to him too!

Dr. Ross   Spicer, if you know why Gordon made his decision then you can start to understand it. With understanding comes acceptance and that's when you and Norma can work to make Gordon's decision the right decision. You can work with Kiko and Anita in figuring out how to give your grandkids the life Gordon and Erica wanted. You can have just as big of stake in their lives as you did before. No one is trying to take that from you.

Kiko   We want you around as much as you want to be around, Mr. Jones. Me and Anita both.

Norma   I'd like to know why, then? I'd like to hear it.

Spicer   This is foolishness. Kiko telling us he wants us around. Him and Anita. Anita, you a sweet woman. I ain't got no problem with either of you. But any day now you two could go your separate ways. Then what? My grandbabies gotta make another adjustment. Me and my wife ain't going nowhere. That's the type of stability a kid needs. Gordon appreciated it. He did. Nah, he ain't show it. But I know it made a difference.

Kiko   You want me to marry Anita? Will that help you accept everything going on? I'll marry her. Hell, I'll marry her right now. (*To* **Anita**.) Baby, marry me! Please. Shit!

Anita   Come on, calm down, Kiko.

Andrea   Daddy, you and Mama staying together all these years is inspiring. Anyone can appreciate that. But it's not the end-all, be-all.

Spicer   Andrea, you don't have kids. Or a man for that matter. Okay? You way out your jurisdiction right now.

Norma   I'd still like to know. If we can get back to that.

Spicer   *Ain't the end-all, be-all.* It's the way it oughta be, damn it. That's what it is. When possible, a kid oughta be raised by blood and damn sure with both parents in the house.

Kiko   Gordon didn't see it that way, Mr. Jones. Otherwise he wouldn't have left them to me.

Spicer   Gordon was probably pissed off that day! Whenever he signed whatever the fuck he signed. He was mad. He was always like that. (*To* **Norma**.) Wasn't he? He'd get mad and make a big decision. Skipped his senior prom cause he got mad at his girlfriend. Regretted it. Showed up late with twenty minutes left. But he can't show up late to this party. He gone. Can't take back what he did. And I haven't fought it have I? I ain't lawyer up even though I could've. You keep talking about accepting it. I've accepted it damn it! But you all want me to be happy about it. Want me to smile from ear to ear.

Dr. Ross   Okay, let's not let this get away from us. This is good though. Let's just dial it back some.

Spicer   And you want to throw it in my face. *Me and Anita want you around. Me and Anita will let you see the kids whenever.* You and Anita! You like saying that shit but there ain't no you and Anita. Y'all boyfriend and girlfriend. That shit ain't real.

Kiko   It's real enough, sir.

Spicer   Yeah, yeah, yeah. I guess so, boy.

Anita   Excuse me, can I ask something? Am I allowed?

Dr. Ross   Of course.

Anita   Mr. Jones, is it that you think you and Mrs. Jones are just the better option or that Kiko and I are unfit?

Norma   No one said anything about being unfit.

Spicer   No I'll answer that. Yes. I do think you're unfit. A man can go out there and earn his money with his own blood, sweat, and tears. See, that gives him the right to spend it. And that makes him better suited to budget it. He's more careful with it. He knows where it came from and how hard it was to get it. But you take that money from him and go give it to another. What the other man care? He ain't work for it. He didn't earn it. Maybe he's careful with it. Maybe he's not. But it ain't his. I put my blood, sweat, and tears into Gordon and his sister. Got them to where they are. Because of that, Gordon could have some kids of his own. That's my blood flowing through them babies. Sure, you love them. I don't doubt that. But you don't deserve them. You able bodied. You're young. Go make some of your own. Go earn your right to have some kids. I done earned mine.

Kiko   So that's what we're talking about? DNA? A ring and a piece of paper that says Anita can have half of my shit? She can have *all* my shit. I'm telling you Mr.

Jones, that ain't what mattered to Gordon. (*Beat.*) Gordon and Erica were going to get a divorce. But you didn't know that did you?

Anita   Kiko, hold on.

Kiko   No, it's the truth. That's what we're all here for. To get to the truth.

Norma   Wait . . . what are you talking about?

Andrea   Yeah, please explain.

Kiko   They had papers worked up and everything. It was going to be amicable. Nothing nasty. Everything done out of love.

Spicer   You a fucking liar, boy!

Kiko   Why would I lie?

Norma   I don't understand. I don't . . . divorce? Why? They never even talked about having problems. Andrea, did they?

Andrea   I knew there were issues. But this is my first time hearing something about divorce.

Spicer   What issues? There's always issues. So what? You taking something he said and running with it, Kiko.

Kiko   They filed papers. There's record of it.

Dr. Ross   Please, everyone let's take a deep breath and try to relax.

Norma   What for, Kiko? What happened?

Kiko   A lot of things, Mrs. Jones. (*Beat.*) Erica was seeing someone else.

Anita   Kiko, baby, stop.

Kiko   She's asking.

Spicer   Erica wasn't that type of woman. She just wasn't.

Kiko   I guess she was provoked. Gordon wasn't perfect. Seemed like he understood why.

Gordon *enters. Everyone looks on as* **Kiko** *interacts with him.*

Gordon   Yeah man. It's the right thing to do, you know. I just never thought we'd end up here. Damn.

Kiko   What are you going to do? Take a paternity test?

Gordon   Hell nah. For what? That's my son. We're too far along now.

Kiko   Why can't you make it work then? You forgave her. She forgave you. Y'all can get through this.

Gordon   Shit, it's gotten too ugly, man. I'm looking in the mirror and seeing something I swore I'd never become. You know? I ain't even mad at her. I mean I am.

But I get it. I broke her heart. Said some shit. Did some shit. Can't open no door and then blame somebody when the cool breeze hits them and they decide to go on outside.

Kiko   What the fuck are you talking about? You sound like your daddy.

Gordon   I grabbed her. Hard. Shook her. Threw her aside. This ain't no metaphor. I put my hands on her. I stood over her. She was scared, Kiko. And I know I'd never do it again. But at one point I knew I'd never do it to begin with. (*Beat.*) It's all love between me and Erica. Maybe somewhere down the line we find out something we don't know now and realize we gotta be together. But right now, we gotta go another way. I ain't gonna let us become my folks. She still got some genuine respect and admiration for me. She still thinks I'm a good man. She still the best woman I ever knew. I wanna preserve that.

He exits.

Spicer   You a damn liar! My boy wouldn't do no shit like that!

Norma   Spicer, calm down.

Spicer   No! He's lying dammit.

Anita   No, he's not.

Spicer   Shut the hell up, little girl.

Andrea   Daddy!

Spicer   Everybody shut up talking to me! Except Kiko. You the only somebody I wanna hear something from. And it better be an apology. Take back that lie you told on my boy!

Kiko   I haven't told a lie.

Spicer   Motherfucker, you think I'm playing with you!

He picks up that rock on the small table. Again, it's heavy but he gets it up above his head. **Dr. Ross** *yells with authority.*

Dr. Ross   Spicer! No!

She runs towards the door yelling at someone down the hall.

Get me security now!

Kiko   See how you're acting? You ain't ever gonna see your grandkids acting like this, man!

Anita   / Mr. Jones, please!

Andrea   Daddy!

Norma   Spicer, stop it! Damn it! You hear me!

Kiko   Mr. Jones, will you just calm the fuck down! What are you doing?!

Spicer *is stalking* **Kiko** *who is evading and has circled behind the couch but in doing so stumbles and falls. We can't see him behind the couch, but we see* **Spicer** *standing over him with the rock above his head. Others plead with him to stop.*

Spicer   I said take back that lie you told on my boy! Take it back or I'll chop your motherfucking ass in half! Take it back!

He throws, with much force, the rock onto **Kiko**.

Scene Seven

Spicer *stands in the same position he was when he previously asked* **Gordon** *what his mother said about the oxtails.* **Gordon** *has just walked out the door, so* **Spicer** *is there alone.* **Norma** *enters from the other side. This is a flashback.*

Norma   Gordon leave?

Spicer   Yeah, he left. He's mad at us.

Norma   I'm mad at him. Talking to us like that. He gets hot and he can't control himself. He gets that from you.

Spicer   Yeah, maybe. I'll talk to him once he cools down.

Norma   Look what I found in the freezer.

She shows him something wrapped in brown butcher paper.

Spicer   What's that?

Norma   The oxtails.

Spicer   I looked in the freezer.

Norma   They were behind that old box of corn dogs the babies didn't want.

Spicer   Who put them there?!

Norma   I honestly don't know. Maybe I did.

Spicer   Hell, it could've been me. I just told the boy you were losing your damn mind over them.

Norma   I was going to tell him the same thing about you.

Spicer   Lord. We both losing our damn minds. He gonna put us in a crazy home.

Norma   And he'd be right.

Spicer   That boy don't pay us no mind. Shit, let him get old. He'll see.

Norma   You gonna call him up and tell him we found them?

Spicer   Nah, what for?

Norma   Cause we didn't have to get him all in the middle of it. Seems like we ruined his day.

Spicer   He'll be alright. He knows us. We ain't mean no harm.

Norma   Yeah, I suppose you're right. Well, you want me to make these oxtails for dinner?

Spicer   Yeah, go ahead.

Norma   It's going to be a while. I gotta make another cake.

Spicer   Norma, now I don't wanna keep talking / about—

Norma   Spicer, dammit, I gotta make it, baby. There's a lot of people expecting it.

Spicer   Alright then.

They begin to walk off.

Hey, why did you make the stew if you never found the oxtails?

Norma   Hell if I know.

They pause.

Spicer   You think we should call him? After all, we were wrong.

Norma   Nah, like you said, he knows us. We were wrong about some oxtails, so what? We ain't perfect. He'll be alright. He'll be just fine.

They both accept this initially, shrug even, as they agree non-verbally that it was no big deal. Then, their faces suddenly go blank and maybe, just maybe, they get it. That it's not okay. And although subtle, it's even more brief, as the lights go to black immediately.

The end.

Mother/son

So what if we don't?
Never see shit the same.
Never relate.
Never ever understand one another.
So what if we don't . . . Mama?

Characters

John *(aka Jah-bo, thirty to forty), Black man*
Lydia *(aka Mama, approx. twenty years older than John), White woman*
Tisha *(thirty to forty), Black woman*

Setting

Patio facing backyard of John's house.

Time

Late fall, 2020.

Slash (/) indicates overlapping dialogue and where the next line should begin. PLEASE be mindful of the slashes before a character's dialogue. Essentially this means the next line should start at the same time and could be a continuation of that character's previous line.

Whereas (Beat.) indicates the speaker taking a moment, ellipsis (. . .) by itself indicates the character is unable to respond and we should see/feel this.

(ʌʌʌ) at the end of the line indicates the next actor should clip this line, not interrupt it. It should be stylized in that the characters are speaking to themselves more than each other and not actually listening. They could even be non-facing.

The Black characters are speaking in Black vernacular—not to be confused with illiteracy or lack of education. For the most part, words aren't misspelled to indicate this. If an actor is struggling with this, they've probably been miscast.

Act One

Scene One

John *and his mother* **Lydia** *sit outside on his patio early morning. The sun has just come up. They look out into his yard which is nice and neat and accessible easily from the patio. She's in a fluffy robe sitting on one side of a patio table. He's on the other side wearing sweats, a tee shirt, and baseball cap. You would never know these two were mother and son. She's nursing some hot tea while he's drinking a big fancy bottled water. She's also supposed to be eating a bowl of something he's concocted. She's not happy about it. He watches her to make sure she eats it; she evades with random convo.*

Lydia   Well, at least it looks like it'll be a pretty day today.

John   Looks like it.

Lydia   I bet you never come out and just sit, do you?

John   Every now and then.

Lydia   I'd be out here every morning.

John   I chill out here sometimes.

Lydia   What, once a month?

John   Mama, I don't know. Just whenever I feel like it.

Lydia   So never?

John   Nah, like I said, every now and then.

Lydia   You never enjoyed the outdoors as much as me and your sister.

John   I enjoyed it—when there was something to do. Playing ball, running around, riding bikes. But just sitting around in it? Nah. I don't like just sitting around nowhere.

Lydia   So, then, you enjoyed playing ball and riding bikes. It wasn't necessarily about the outdoors.

John   Okay, Mama, whatever you say.

Lydia   When you like the outdoors you can come out and just smell the dew and wet grass first thing in the morning. No filler needed. (*Beat.*) I like your deck. You got a good deck for smelling dew. You got a pretty yard, too. You hire a landscaper?

John   Nah, I did it myself.

Lydia   *You* did your own yard? You hated yard work growing up. You hated work, period. Anything that required you using your hands.

John   Yeah, let you and Pops tell it.

Lydia   Is there someone who can tell it differently?

John   You oughta put the tea down and eat a little bit.

Lydia   I am.

John   You ain't touched it.

Lydia   I took a bite.

John   Mama, that spoon ain't been moved.

Lydia   Goddammit, here you go. Don't sit here and act like you remember the exact angle of the spoon.

John   I do. Just in case you tried to pull this shit. I counted the berries too. Ten. Ten of them little motherfuckers. How many you think are left?

Lydia   I don't know and I don't give a shit. And you need to watch your mouth, *Mr. Grown Man.*

John   Count 'em. *One, two, three / four, five . . .*

Lydia   That's real chicken-shit, you know that? I'm trying to be civil and you wanna prove me up every chance you get. I'm telling / you I took a bite.

John   *six, seven / eight, nine, TEN!*

She digs into the bowl with an urgency and takes a big bite and talks with her mouth full.

Lydia   Here I'll take another bite! Okay?! That better?! Huh? I'll eat this lumpy, cold shit.

John   It used to be hot. It got cold sitting here while you talked about the smell of dew and wet grass.

Lydia   Excuse the hell out of me. You're too good for pleasantries?

John   Not at all. But pleasantries came at the expense of some hot oatmeal. That's all I'm saying. It wasn't always cold. I gave it to you—it was hot.

Lydia   You smug bastard. Just like your dad.

She contemplates taking another bite but decides not to after swirling the spoon around in disgust.

Would it have killed you to make it with some goddamn toppings? That's how I use to make yours. Butter. Brown sugar. Walnuts.

John   What you think the berries are for?

Lydia   Oooh big fucking deal. Bitter ass blueberries. I hate blueberries. You know that. You ever see me sitting around eating blueberries? I'm telling you I can't eat this watery shit. You could've at least used milk.

John   You said milk does you bad.

Lydia   The milk cooks out, Einstein.

John   You telling me if I use milk to make you some oatmeal, the dairy, or lactose, whatever it is that fucks you up / cooks out?

Lydia   I said watch your mouth!

John   Milk is milk. Cooked or not. You said it does you bad.

Lydia   Cause you offered me some warm milk when I couldn't sleep. I can't sit up and drink a whole glass of milk that late.

John   Yeah, well . . . I couldn't very well go out there and score you a crack rock to soothe you over could I, Mama?

Lydia   You go to hell.

A moment.

John   You talk to Pops?

Lydia   Yeah.

John   What he talking about?

Lydia   Ain't nothing new. This. That. I know you talked to him too.

John   Yeah. But we don't talk about what y'all talk about.

Lydia   That should tell you not to ask about it then.

John   I was just making conversation. *Pleasantries*, remember?

Lydia   You wanna know when he wants me back home. That's what you're digging for.

John   Yeah that too.

Lydia   Well, he doesn't. Not yet.

John   That's fine.

Lydia   Yeah, you say that now. *Sure, Mom, stay here as long as you'd like. Stay here at my house while I treat you like a goddamn prisoner!*

John   Talking about watching my mouth. Matter fact when you at my house no more blasphemy. There's my first rule. If you a prisoner then I'm the warden. The sheriff. The boss. Yeah, I'm in charge here. (*Beat.*) Them tables sure do turn sometimes, don't they, Mama?

Lydia   Oh / please!

John   You heard what I said.

Lydia   Get over yourself! *I* taught *you* about God. Don't preach to me, boy.

He doesn't allow even a split second to pass before jumping on that.

John   Don't call me that shit.

Lydia   Whatever.

John   Yeah, *whatever*. Just don't call me that shit. I don't let people call me that. Call me John, call me son, call me Jah-bo. But I ain't nobody's boy.

Lydia   You're my boy.

John   I said I ain't nobody's.

Lydia   Well, I'm your mother.

John   Yeah, my ol' white ass mama.

Lydia   Jesus, you know what—am I gonna get clean eventually? You betcha! But my God, son, what are you going to do about the bullshit you're on?

John   What am I on, Mama? Huh?

Lydia   You tell me.

John   No, I wanna hear you say it. Call it. Give it a name. What? I'm on this *Black* bullshit. *Negro* bullshit. / Cause I don't want you to call me boy?

This infuriates her.

Lydia   I've never in my goddamn life said something like that! I gotta Black son. A Black daughter. A Black husband. I've never said it. I never thought it. I never! Period.

John   Well, I don't know what you're talking about then. I only asked you not to call me boy and you called it *bullshit*. But it seems like an easy enough thing to understand. You got Black kids, like you say. A Black husband. Seems like a sensible thing to ask of someone like you. Don't call me boy in no condescending, white ass way.

Lydia   Fine, son.

John   Yeah, fine. Go ahead and eat that oatmeal. You didn't eat nothing all day yesterday. You ain't going to be here smoking cigarettes, drinking pop, and eating chocolate pie all day. You need some whole foods. Nutrients. Your body's just a factory for poison right now. And then got the nerve to wonder why you feel like shit all the damn time.

Lydia   I said I'll eat it. Just . . . get away from me. Go inside or something. I don't want you looking at me. Go find something to do.

John   I found something.

Lydia   It ain't watching me.

John   It's *watching over* you.

Lydia   Ha! Yeah, really?

John   Really.

Lydia   Sure, it is.

John   That's what this whole thing is.

Lydia   What thing?

John   *What thing?* Boy, I'll tell you, the whole little naïve shit you do all the time, it's nerve-racking as hell.

Lydia   I just asked a damn question. What *thing*? What is this thing about? You referenced it, not me.

John   You got Pops around your finger. Jazzy can't tell you *no* to save her life. So, here we are. You and me. Cause I'm unaffected by your manipulation. I'm trying to help you. That's the thing.

Lydia   I don't manipulate your father or your sister. I talk to them; they listen to me. Oh they don't really give a damn about me; I'm not in la-la-fucking-land when it comes to them either. But they don't hate me like you do. They gotta heart.

John   Yeah so do I.

Lydia   And it's an icy son of a bitch.

John   Be that as it may, you're here so I can watch over you. Tell you *no*. And to tell you what to do. Cause being left up to your own discretion your decisions have been pretty fucked-up, right?

Lydia   ...

John   Right.

Lydia   Just take me to rehab. Take me anywhere. I want to get as far away from you as possible. I can't stand it. I can't stand being here. Under your reign of fucking terror. You fucking hate me, Goddamn tyrant!

John   It's been a few days, Mama. I think you'll survive.

Lydia   And I bet that just kills you, don't it?

John   Why would I let you stay here? Huh? If that's the case.

Lydia   So you can pat yourself on your back. Tell your dad how good you are to me despite *all the horrible, despicable, torturous things* I did to you. How I ruined your life.

He's emphatically agreeing with what she's saying sarcastically.

John   Hell yeah!

Lydia   Oh please. If I need rehab you certainly need a shrink, kid.

John   Agreed.

Lydia   You give your dad any of this bullshit?

John   I don't have to. He's owned up to it . . . somewhat.

Lydia   And I haven't?

John   When?

Lydia   All the goddamn time!

John   Please! You're on drugs, Mama. Drugs! You haven't acknowledged that one time but wanna find ways to blame everyone else for it. Ain't said sorry or even looked like those words were anywhere on your face. Even after all the lies, all the manipulation, all the money you've stolen. How much money you done stole from me, huh?

Lydia   Not a fucking dime!

John   When you ask me for money and say it's for one thing and it ain't—it's stealing.

Lydia   It's lying! It ain't stealing!

John   And all of a sudden those things are different?

Lydia   Yeah, whatever.

John   *If you'll lie, you'll steal.* Right, Mama?

Lydia   That's right, son. That is absolutely right. I instilled values in you. Truths. So what if I didn't always abide by them? I told you the right thing. Or what? I should've shoved cigarettes down your throat too? *Here you go, baby boy, smoke up, you little shithead. Mama smokes so she can't tell you not to!*

He laughs in disbelief.

John   Yeah alright, Mama.

Lydia   No, really. You'd be the person calling me a no-good bitch for giving my life jacket to you and putting you back on the boat as the current ripped me away. *But you don't have your life jacket on, Mama!* Well, you know what son, tough shit! We're in different rooms, on different boards, playing different games. I don't have to abide by the same rules. (*Beat.*) Ungrateful! That's what you are.

John   You're serious?

Lydia   As a heart attack. I give you life lessons and you resent me for it. Mad because I held you to a standard.

John   A standard you're somehow exempt from? It's okay for you to lie and steal from family? That ain't a universal rule?

Lydia   Jesus, so you gave me . . . what? A few hundred dollars? I'll pay it back. Alright?

John   Pay me back with what money? Huh? Your ass ain't about to get a job. You'd let Pops get out there in hundred-degree weather with a bad back, bad knee, and bad heart and have him lifting and pulling and dragging shit around at seventy-two before you get a job at the grocery store a few hours a day.

Lydia   I can't work!

John   Entitled than a motherfucker.

Lydia   God damn you!

John   Talking about paying me back. Well, you can't pay me back in oxycodone. No, ma'am. That's you and your friends' kinda currency, not mine.

Lydia   I can come up with a few hundred dollars.

John   A few hundred?

Lydia   Five, six . . . I don't know.

John   Try ten or eleven *thousand*.

Lydia   Bullshit!

John   And if you add the money I spent getting you things you could've bought for yourself, if you wasn't putting it up your nose—fifteen, sixteen thousand maybe.

Lydia   Fuck you! Sixteen thousand, my ass!

John   How would you know?

Lydia   I know.

John   I went into savings. Used up credit cards. Loaned against my 401k. For what I thought was your mortgage. Hospital bills. Pop's prescriptions. All the while you been fucking high, Mama. You don't know your ass from a hole in the ground. Let alone how much money you've stolen from me.

Lydia   Goddammit now, I'm serious. Stop saying I stole it. I didn't climb through your window. Or pick your locks. Or snatch it out your hands.

John   Not literally.

Lydia   Literally, figuratively, or any other damn way.

John   You're a liar, Mama. A thief and an addict, too. What you say, at any given moment, don't mean shit. You can't say you didn't steal something based on your own logic. Your logic is some decrepit, dysfunctional shit right now.

Lydia   Call your dad and tell him to pick me up! And if he won't I'll walk out. I'll walk out there, live on the streets, and get ran over by a semi before I stand here and let you talk to me like this. I'm your mother, you little judgmental son of a bitch.

John   *Son of a bitch.* Yeah, I'm assuming you don't see the irony in that.

Lydia   I see it. I see it just fine. And I stand by it. I'm a real bitch spawning something like you. I bet none of your friends treat their mother this way.

John   Probably don't.

Lydia   Yeah, I know they don't.

He tries to irritate her at this point.

John   They got Black mamas who wouldn't take that shit. I guess that's just the white boy in me. My cracker side.

Lydia I'll get your *Black dad* to come over here and kick the white side of your ass then.

John He'd probably try it too. That nigga loves standing up for his woman.

Lydia You know what? You and that mouth. You say something like that to me again and I'm going to smack you right in it. And if you wanna hit me back then do it. Throw me. Punch me. Kill me. I don't care, but that's what you'll have to do because I won't tolerate it.

John And what am I supposed to tolerate, Mama? Whatever you throw my way?

Lydia I never asked you to do that. I didn't ask to be here.

John . . .

Lydia Did I? Did I call you? Did I come knocking at your door? You told me last February that I wasn't shit and to never call you again and I haven't, have I?

John I never said that. I ain't ever said you weren't shit. I said you don't know shit.

Lydia Oh, *and all of a sudden those things are different?* (*Beat.*) I didn't ask to be here.

John Pops asked.

Lydia And you'd do anything for him. Nothing for me. Your old hoe of a mother. But anything for him.

John He didn't ask me to do it for him. Or you. Or for me. He asked me to do it for *us*. Me, Jazzy, you, and him, the four of us, we use to be something. A good thing. Might've even called us a real family.

He contemplates a bit, loses all of the aggression. Laughs to himself even thinking about something.

I remember when Grandma was getting that procedure done, for . . . what was that? Her kidney?

Lydia Yeah.

John My freshman year in college, right?

Lydia Sophomore.

John Sophomore?

Lydia Yeah. You was dating Nora. She wanted to be there but had to work. She stopped by the visiting room with donuts for all of us though. Charmed the shit out of your dad. That was your sophomore year because I told you I wasn't crazy about her and you gave me your *I'm twenty and can date who I want speech*. Right before you moved to Chicago.

John Yeah, that sounds about right. Anyways, we were all at the hospital. All of your brothers and sisters, most of the grandchildren. Up there pulling for her; we were there all day. About thirty of us spread out in the waiting room and everyone found a little corner they congregated to. But it was me and you, Pops and Jazzy sitting and playing cards with Uncle Beeno, Leslie, Travis . . .

Lydia   Clint. He was sitting over there with us too.

John   That's right. But the four of us, we were talking shit to each other. Nonstop. You know how we do. At one point it's me and Pops talking shit to you and Jazzy, then boom! Pops and Jazzy talking shit on me. Then boom! Me and Pops talking shit on her. You would co-sign pretty much with everyone. Kept it neutral. But we could never really pull you all the way in, to tell the truth. You'd laugh. You'd slip a few smart-ass things in there. But for the most part you were . . . I don't know . . . I guess, just the peacekeeper.

Lydia   It's hard for you to say anything good about me anymore, ain't it?

John   Nah. It's not hard to say it, Mama. It's hard on me to have to remember it. I mean I see it, can still hear it. It's all vivid. But it's hard it has to be a memory. Probably a moment we'll never have again. Anyways, Uncle Beeno hears us all talking shit and he was just staring at us. And he goes—*I just love the way all of you are together*. Of course, Pops thought he was talking shit so he told him go to hell. But Uncle Beeno says *no, I'm serious. The way you all interact. Weave in and out with one another, the jokes, the shit talking, the conversation, the affection, and all that, you all are just so familiar with each other.* And we were. And us being familiar with each other seems familiar within itself, but it's been so motherfucking long.

Lydia   Let me guess, because of me.

John   Mama, I'm trying to really talk to you right now. But if you're going to keep on being aloof and keep on refusing to see how your behavior and the things you've done has impacted this family, then I'm not going to keep trying.

She gets up and wanders about the deck. She pulls a pack of cigarettes out her pocket. She holds one in between her fingers and waves it in front of **John**, *flippantly, for his "permission." He nods his approval. She lights it and stares out into the yard.*

Lydia   And why are you trying? Why now?

John   . . .

Lydia   Why talk to me now? I mean, for Christ sakes, it's been a year and half since we spoke a single word to each other?

John   Since last February, yeah.

Lydia   Two of your birthdays. Two of mine. Christmases and Thanksgivings. Two Mother's Days. That one really hurt. Did you even consider picking up the phone and calling me?

John   No.

Lydia   Wow. Thanks for indulging me.

John   I'm not here to indulge you, Mama. I ain't got shit for you but the truth. At every turn and every corner, no matter how sad it might be or how bad you might want a little sweet lie to lift your spirits up. You ask me, I'll tell you.

Lydia   Then why? Why give me all that shit about how and what we used to be? We *used* to be a lot of things. I used to be young and pretty. Your dad used to make up nicknames for me. You used to suck on the tit.

He grimaces.

John   Oh come on, Mama. Shit.

Lydia   Oh what, that's not a *truth* you want to talk about?

Damn near too disgusted to string a sentence together.

John   I don't . . . no . . . absolutely not. I never ever want to think or talk about that for the rest of my fucking life, Mama.

Lydia   Accusing me of being manipulative; look at you. Going down memory lane just so when you tell me what to do, I can think it's coming from a place of love. But I see how you look at me, it ain't lovingly.

John   Where's it coming from then?

Lydia   That's what am asking you. What? Why? Why now? It ain't for things to be how they used to be; things won't ever be like that again. Hell, even I know that. (*Beat.*) Can you ever see yourself hugging me again? Huh? When's the last time you even hugged your mama?

John   . . .

Lydia   What if I came over there right now and hugged you? What would you do? If I hugged my son. My grown son. Who I carried. Who I birthed. Nobody ever thought you were more beautiful than me. What would you do?

John   . . .

Lydia   You wouldn't hug me back, that's for sure. You'd stand there. You'd clam up. Unsure of where to put your hands. Like I was a piece of trash you didn't want to sully yourself with. I'd tell you I love you and you'd say *yeah, okay, Mama. Okay.*

John   . . .

Lydia   Or what, am I wrong?

She takes a few steps towards him indicating she's about to see what he'd do if she hugged him.

John   Go on somewhere, Mama.

Lydia   You fucking hate me so much.

John   You keep saying that.

Lydia   You ain't said I was wrong.

John   You got your mind made up.

Lydia   Let's see. Tell me I'm wrong. Tell me how much you love your mama. I'm listening . . .

John   . . .

Lydia   That's what I thought.

John   You need to eat that goddamn oatmeal.

Lydia   Ooohhh listen to you. I thought we don't talk like that here. *Warden. Sheriff. Boss.* Mama still knows how to get to you, huh? Ha! Just a little punk still.

John   Yeah alright. If I were out there somewhere and some nigga called me that I'd bust his head in.

Lydia   I'm shivering.

John   If you really knew me you would be.

Lydia   You threatening me, son? Really?

He realizes she has made him act in a way he doesn't want to; he'd never threaten nor think about hurting his mother. He checks himself, turns his frown into a forced smile.

John   Nah, I ain't threatening you, Mama. I'll leave before I let you turn me into something like that. You're my mother still, I'll concede that.

Lydia   And me being your mother means something to you? Oh please.

John   What's me being your son mean?

Lydia   It means I wouldn't stand here implying that I'd bust your head open. And that's what you just had the audacity to say to me.

John   I was just letting you know you getting more leniency than the average person . . . because you're my mother. And if you knew me you'd know that.

Lydia   Well, be my guest, beat my ass. Show me how big and bad you are. I make one call to your dad, bad back and bad knee and all and he'd come over here and smack you with a two-by-four if he knew you were disrespecting me. (*Beat.*) *If I knew you.* Dare I say no one knows you better?

John   Why cause you're my mother?

Lydia   Precisely.

John   Nah, you're just *Lydia*. I ain't got no mama. She been gone and even she didn't know much. She never cared to.

Lydia   That's fine, son. Call me by my name. Call me whatever. Won't change the fact I'm still your mother. You came from me.

John   Ain't about where you're from but it's about where you're going, thank God.

Lydia   Yeah, okay. And where are you headed? Who have you become? You're so proud that you summoned up the courage to talk to me how you're talking to me. Cussin'. Not caring. Disrespecting me. You wasn't raised like that. Where you were from, you talked to me and your dad right. Talked right about yourself. Now, you just

want to prove to everyone how goddamn bold you are. And you know what, I'll go
ahead and say it . . . if you want to know the truth . . .

John   The *truth*?! Are you capable of that?

Lydia   I sure am. You want to prove how *Black* you are. Ever since you went to
Chicago. Came back trying to convince everyone you're someone new. *I'm Jah-bo
this. Jah-bo that. What up, nigga, it's me, Jah-bo! Nigga. Nigga / Nigga.*

John   Whoa! There she goes. Finally, huh? You got your little white mouth around
that word real fucking easy, didn't you, Mama? Let's be honest, you've said it a
million times.

Lydia   I'm quoting you.

John   Nah you ain't quoting me. You found an opening and took it. Scratched that
surface to reveal your true colors. Didn't take much scratching, it was a shallow
surface anyways. Most folks could see through it.

Lydia   Oh what are you talking about now? Huh? I don't have any true colors. What
you see is what you get.

John   Yeah I guess that's true. Cause I sure saw you calling every Jorge, Jesus, Jose,
and Miguel *wetback* this and *wetback* that. *Chink*, *wop*, *dago*, all that shit. I won't
believe for a second you drew the line at *nigger*.

Lydia   How can you talk to me like this? All of sudden I'm a racist now too?

John   Not all of a sudden, no. You always been it. I always seen the signs.

Lydia   What signs, John? Was it me hugging and kissing all your little friends when
they came over? Fixing you all snacks and buying pizzas and sending them money for
their birthdays? They called me mama and I treated them like sons. And not one of
them was white. Was that a sign? Or every little girl you brought by the house, bless
their hearts, some of them were the cutest, sweetest little things, and sure some of
them I didn't care for, but it wasn't because they were Black. I always treated them
good. I didn't have any signs. I don't have no true colors to reveal. And if you say
otherwise then you're the fucking liar.

John   You sitting up tabulating every decent deed or interaction you had with my
Black friends seems to be a sign all on its own. All the while I was tallying up every
cringeworthy thing you did.

Lydia   What cringeworthy shit did I do?

John   Hell, where to begin, Mama? What about when Keisha came by and had
started her locs and you told her she looked so much prettier when it was straight.

Lydia   I said she looked pretty either way, but I liked the other way.

John   Or when you told Jeff his son was so adorable with his little *jet-black ass.*

Lydia   It was a joke! Obviously, the kid is gorgeous.

John   It's fucking ignorant. And embarrassing. And telling. You told on yourself. You fixed snacks and sent birthday cards with a few bucks to try and prove something to *you*; but you are who you are. (*Beat.*) What about how you told all your brothers and sisters how *John and Jazzy don't date white people. I guess they don't realize they're just as much Irish as they are Black.* Yeeeaaah . . . oh what? You didn't think that got back to me?

Lydia   Well, neither you nor your sister ever dated anyone white and my side of the family is Irish. Where's the lie?

John   Irish my motherfucking ass! You don't know a damn thing about Ireland, Irish culture, Irish people; hell, the fighting Irish or Irish motherfucking cream. Shit. Me and Jazzy supposed to embrace your daddy's heritage? A man we never saw and the only thing we ever heard about him was he was a deadbeat. Your ass got some nerve, disrespecting Ireland like that. They're a strong people. Resilient people. Your daddy didn't have none of that.

Lydia   All I said was you didn't date white people!

John   You were castigating. You meant it as an insult. It was airing out a grievance. But you know, you were right. I don't fuck with white women. Only thing I want white on my woman is her teeth and the whites in her eyes.

Lydia   So sorry I ruined a whole population of women for you, son.

John   Shit, I'm not.

Lydia   I'll own up to a lot of things. If you wanna call me an addict, fine. A horrible mother, I guess I don't have a choice but to concede; that's your call to make. But I ain't no racist. I had every right to have the kids I had with who I chose to have them with. You may hate that you gotta old white ass mama but it's the hand you were given. But I ain't no racist.

John   You just said *nigga nigga nigga.* Did you not?

Lydia   I was just saying that's all I've heard you say since I've been here.

John   Yeah, well I can say it. I'm Black.

Lydia   And white.

John   I'm Black.

Lydia   You're mixed.

John   Brownies are mixed too. Milk, eggs, butter, all type of shit, all mixed in there. But it don't take but that one scoop of cocoa and you gotta brownie. Brown. Dark brown. Light brown. Chocolatey brown. *Brownie.* Not a *mixed confection*, or a flour-cocoa treat, but a rich, chocolate, decadent brownie. That's what they call it cause that's what it is. Just like you said, the milk and all that other shit cooks out.

Lydia   Okay, whatever, *Jah-bo.*

John   Damn right. That is certainly what they call me.

Lydia   You know, it's not just me who feels like this. Your dad does too.

John   Pops feels like what?

Lydia   He feels the same way I do. About you. Your alter ego. Who you've become.

John   Woman, you so far out your mind. You can't tell me shit about him. Me and my father talk.

Lydia   I know you do.

John   Nah you don't know. You think you know. You know he calls me and I call him but you don't know what we talk about or to what extent. You think you still know him better than me and I'm telling you if you do, if you think that, then you here on Earth and your mind is lightyears away, just a bunch of mush, too far to ever come back.

Lydia   John, I've been with the man longer than you been alive. Unlike you and Tisha, we made it work. Ha! He ain't gonna show you everything he shows me. Especially about you, he don't want to push you away.

John   More manipulation. This late in the game? You gonna lay that manipulation card down hard and ride it out ain't you?

Lydia   I'm laying down what I know is true.

John   That Pops has a problem with who I am? The man I turned out to be?

Lydia   He has his concerns, sure.

John   Bullshit.

Lydia   I mean, if you don't / want to believe me . . .

John   Bullshit, woman! (*Beat.*) Here's the motherfucking skinny, you woke up one day, in one of your few moments of clarity and realized you didn't know who the fuck your own son is. You spent your whole life assuming you knew him, that he belonged to you, that he would be who you said he was and you missed his whole journey. Everyone's changing, Mama. Evolving. Pops ain't gotta problem with who I am. He done changed some too. He ain't run into no brick wall when it comes to who I am, it ain't hit him out of nowhere. He's been right beside me the whole time. I've been Jah-bo. I've been John. They all the same, you just don't know either one.

Lydia   Well, all I know is I've asked your dad where did all this . . .

She points at him up and down signifying everything she sees when she looks at him.

Where did this come from? The walk, the way you talk, the politics, the conspiracy theories, the whole nine. I asked him and he said he don't know either.

John   Well, I believe that. He was pacifying you. You probably asked him in the middle of the night and all he wanted to do was sleep. What was he supposed to say? *This is our son, Lydia. This is him as a man, not our puppet.* Was he supposed to tell you that you fried your mind and can't see a damn thing?

Lydia   . . . I wasn't doing this shit when you were growing up.

John   So you say.

Lydia   I wasn't!

John   Then that's unfortunate. Because that means you don't have anything to blame. I started becoming a man I could be proud of and you decided to look away.

Lydia   I didn't decide anything. You didn't want to include me.

John   I wanted you there. I ain't always push you away. I used to be playful with you. Come into the house and pick you up and spin you around once I got bigger than you. Run up to you after every race in high school, put my arm around you and yell out *this my mama! The crazy white lady is mine y'all! And I love her!* But at some point I needed more from you than just a mother who wanted to baby me. I offered you that position, Mama, to be a friend, a confidante, a counselor, but it required you accepting the fact I'm gonna do some things you may not agree with, so you turned it down.

Lydia   I didn't turn shit down.

John   You turned me down. I literally asked you, Mama—I told you, I need you to be my friend too and you said *I don't want to be your goddamn friend. I'm your mother.* That's what you said.

Lydia   I don't remember that.

John   Of course you don't. But I do. And I knew then what it was all about. See, you right, you're my mother. Ain't neither one of us making it into any history books, but if we did, in a thousand years it would read that you were my mother. The only one I ever had. Nothing you can do, or I can do, or anyone can do to change that. So, you hold on to it because you ain't gotta work for that. Steal from me, you're still my mother. Lie to me, you're still my mother. Lie on me, you're still my mother. Hate everything about me, you're still my mother. It don't take any work. Takes work to be a good one, but good or bad, you still get to wear that hat. But to be a friend? A confidante? A counselor? That shit takes work, don't it, Mama? And you don't work for shit. Cause you're an entitled, selfish, narcissistic ass woman.

Lydia   And you're my judge, right?

John   Nah I never / said that.

Lydia   Yeah you are. Cause you placed yourself so far above me. You're so much better than me. Never would do the things I do. Hell, you're right up there with God. You and Him, looking down on all of us. But watch your step, son. I'd hate to see you make the wrong move because it'll be a long drop. *Mr. Perfect.*

John   I sure never said was perfect.

Lydia   Well, in whatever ways you aren't I bet that's my fault. Right? (*Beat.*) It can't be easy for you to look at me, your *wretched ass mother.* I know that. But I wasn't like this while you were growing up. You had a decent environment.

John   Did I?

Lydia   Yeah, you did.

John   And what qualifies that, Mama?

Lydia   Oh what, you had a terrible childhood now?

John   It wasn't easy.

Lydia   I didn't say it was easy. But it wasn't so bad either.

John   It was dysfunctional, Mama. It's a place I would never want my kids to grow up in.

Lydia   There were bad times. I'm not arguing that. But it wasn't just on me. It was your dad too.

John   I know this.

Lydia   And we made up for a lot of it.

John   Made up how? You two would fight like rabid animals. Say things, disgusting things—wishing death on each other. Things I would never say to another fucking human being. Did it all in front of me and Jazzy and then never let us address it, or express feelings about it or helped us process it. You'd just buy me a new video game and Jazzy some new clothes and hoped we forgot about it.

Lydia   And I don't remember either of you turning it down.

John   That's how you rationalize it?

Lydia   Why are you having this talk with just me? Why not me *and* your dad?

John   I've talked about it with him.

Lydia   And what'd he say? That it was hell putting up with me.

John   Yeah, that. And that he knows it was fucked-up but he was too ashamed to talk to us. Didn't have the words. That he always hoped I forgave him regardless of him asking me to.

Lydia   And how do you know I don't feel the same way he does?

John   You don't know shame, Mama.

Lydia   Oh I know it. I know it well. I see it on your face. On your sister's. On your dad's. All of you are ashamed of me. I've always seen it. You all let each other get away with shit. And when I tried to slide by I get called out. It got hung over my head. I'm the bitch who ruined her kids' lives and her husband's. Who don't understand them. Was I never worth being understood, though? Where's my grace? I'm. Sick. Son. This shit is hard and I'm trying and instead of looking up and seeing my son reaching out his hand to pull me up I see him waving his finger in my face. Jesus, maybe I didn't have the right to be with your dad. To have you all as my kids. Is that what this is about? Why you disown me? I'm just some strung-out white woman that you'll never see eye to eye with?

John   More manipulation! Gaslighting 101! It don't work on me, Mama. How many times I gotta tell you?

Lydia   I'm not trying to work you over. You're going on and on about me not wanting to be beside you on whatever damn journey you're on. Not accepting you. Maybe you haven't accepted me. You always had more in common with your dad. You can look at him and see yourself in one way or another. I don't know, maybe I'm too *woman*. Too old. Too white. Maybe we're too different to ever understand a fucking thing about each other.

John   Mama, I could be pale as you. With thin pink lips. Blonde hair and blue eyes. Hell, I could be a woman named Lydia. Doing the whitest of all perceived white things and you and I still wouldn't see eye to eye. Not because you're an addict but because you have no remorse for being one. No remorse for how far you'll go to stay one. Then you wanna blame somebody else for it all. Whatever the fuck you're on, that's your God now and you'd steal for it. Kill for it. Lie for it. You don't know shit about the real God or anyone you say you love anymore. You just use them. Eat off them. Chew on them until you bite through the fucking core and leave 'em with nothing but a stem. I hate that about you. *That* is what I hate. Not that you're white and by default I'm half white or part white or however you wanna break it down. I know what I am and who I am and I'm good with it. I surely don't hate that you're a woman. It ain't about that. It ain't a white thing. Or a Black thing. Or anything in between. You're just a rotten person. It's a humanity thing. A decency thing. And you ain't got none of that left.

Scene Two

Lydia *has remained outside on the patio. The sun has fully risen and you can tell it's midday.* **John** *comes back out with a gym bag in tow.*

John   You gonna stay out here all day?

Lydia   Maybe. Why not?

John   Well, I'm about to go to the gym. Won't be gone long.

Lydia   Yeah. Great. Have fun.

John   You gonna be alright by yourself?

Lydia   Been by myself a very long time, son.

John   Yeah, well you ain't been here by yourself.

Lydia   I'm not gonna rob you, John. Jesus Christ. Alright? I'll be right here when you get back. Don't believe me? Lock me out. I'll stay right here.

John   Ain't nobody said nothing about that.

Lydia   You were thinking it.

John   How you know what I'm thinking, Mama?

Lydia   ...

John   Look, you got some sweats or something?

Lydia   Why?

John   Just ... do you got any?

Lydia   I brought this robe, some jeans and a few tee shirts.

John   I know you used to like walking. You can jump on the treadmill or bike while I work out for a little while. We can stop and buy you some sweats.

Lydia   Yeah, no thank you. I don't want to walk.

John   May not want to but it could be good for you. Maybe that's why your back and legs hurt all the time. It ain't being put to use.

Lydia   My back hurts because I fell down some goddamn stairs.

John   But maybe you never worked it back up to full strength. I'm just saying a little activity could help.

Lydia   Maybe, I don't know. Not gonna find out either.

John   Alright, figured I'd ask.

Lydia   Don't act like you really wanted me to go.

John   I invited you.

Lydia   Knowing I'd say no.

John   I ain't know what the hell you'd say, Mama. I don't pretend to know you that well.

Lydia   You knew I wasn't going to the gym just like I knew you didn't want me to go.

John   Alright, Mama.

Lydia   You're going to stand there and tell me with a straight face that you wouldn't have been embarrassed to be seen with me? At the gym, around all your little workout buddies. Please!

John   Hell, yeah, I would've been embarrassed, look at you. You're falling apart. Long ass, scraggly, unkempt hair. Limping around like you're thirty years older than you are. There's some women at the gym who could be your mother who run and skip and jump. Yeah I would've been embarrassed.

Lydia   You're such a bastard.

John   But I was also embarrassed of myself the first time I went to the gym. Fifteen-year-olds were in there lifting more than me. Day two I felt a little better. Day three a little better than that and then finally I felt like I belonged. You gonna have to start somewhere, Mama. You can sit out here all day, day after day, having your little friends sneak you over pills to pop here and there when I go to work. Oh yeah, I know about them fucking losers. Or you can take just one step: one step towards something better. Take two tomorrow. Then you look up one day and realize it was never about if other folks were embarrassed of you; but you ain't embarrassed of yourself no more.

Lydia   Duly noted, son. Duly fucking noted. I feel really inspired.

He goes back inside to leave. He's gone for just a few moments before he storms back out to the patio and puts his gym bag down. He pulls a chair up right beside his mother. This is the closest they've been.

John   When's the last time you had a civil conversation?

Lydia   Oh, I don't know. Hell, I don't know when the last time I've been in a civil environment.

John   See, that's what I'm saying. I can ask you the most simple shit and you reply with condescension, sarcasm, manipulation.

Lydia   Hey, don't fucking attack me! I've been out here minding my business. You said you were going to the gym so just go why don't you?!

John   Because I want to have a conversation. A civil one. One that starts at one place and ends in another.

Lydia   We don't have those type of conversations.

John   I agree. So, it's about time we did. (*Beat.*) Do you want to get clean, Mama?

Lydia (*aggravated*)   I'm here, aren't I?

John   No, see, that's what I mean. It's a fair question. I asked it earnestly and you can't help but to reply with your jaws locked and ready to bite.

Lydia   Fair question, my ass. I don't give a shit if it was asked earnestly. I don't care if you asked it while feeding me an ice cream sundae and talking baby-talk. It's offensive regardless. Yeah I want to get clean. What else would I want?

John   I don't see the urgency from you. Or any indication that this is a serious issue or that you need to do better. This isn't *should you cut back on coffee or not*, Mama. And you just shrug your shoulders like it ain't fucking us all up one way or another.

Lydia   Jesus, I'm not smoking crack, son.

John   So then there's a little bit of denial?

Lydia   Yeah. I'm denying that I'm smoking crack.

John   But are you denying this is a serious thing we're dealing with?

Lydia   Compared to crack it isn't, yeah. I'll deny that.

John   . . .

Lydia   I didn't wake up one morning and say *well, hell, I guess I can start abusing my pain medication.* But it happened. And once in a while, once every blue fucking moon, when I need something and I don't have any pills, yeah, I'll bump a line or two. You wanna stand over me and rub my face in it? Fine. I'm a lowlife. *Yada yada yada.*

John   You trying to beat me to the punch, Mama, not knowing that I'm not trying to take it there. Ain't nobody called you nothing besides what you are. You're an addict. That ain't no more a judgment than calling you white, calling Pops Black, or Jazzy tall.

Lydia   I ain't just an *addict* as you say. You don't have to see the trillion other things I am. I don't expect you to. You're just my son. And what's more, a son who ever since I could remember cringed at the possibilities.

John   Possibilities of what?

Lydia   Of me being youthful. Flirty. Young. Ambitious. Pretty. I was just twenty-one when I had you. All of sudden I look up and I can't be me anymore. Because if I joked, I embarrassed you and your dad. If I sung, I embarrassed you. If I danced. You two thought I was some off-beat, big mouth white woman but other people liked me. They did. Your friends even liked me more than you. One day I looked at you and saw your jaw tighten up; you cringed at me, for no other reason than it was me. I thought to myself *well, his dad'll be happy.*

John   Pops ain't got nothing to do with you and me.

Lydia   Of course he does.

John   Pops ain't got no more to do with you and me than you do when it comes to me and him.

Lydia   I got everything to do with you and your father being how you are! I made sure I got out the way. I laid low and he stood tall even if he had his foot on my fucking back.

John   See, and that's where you just don't get it. Both of you think you did a good job keeping shit from me and Jazzy. You think there's things we didn't see. It's the other way around. There's things we know that you don't know we do. Me and Pops are *me and Pops* because I decided a long time ago to judge him only on how he was with me. And I extended that same courtesy to you. He took advantage of it, you didn't.

Lydia   What in the fuck does that even mean? I was never aware of no goddamn courtesy.

A moment of contemplation; he may even chuckle to himself realizing what he's about to say. Though it isn't funny, it's a type of pathetic that renders desperate chuckles.

John   Pops used to always order a big ol' barbecue platter every time me and Tisha would come over; remember that?

Lydia   Yeah—ribs, beef, ham; had enough for days. So what?

John   And then he stopped.

Lydia   Because it gave us food poison last time we got it.

John   Did it?

Lydia   Well, I felt a little funny, but Tisha had to leave the table she was so sick.

John   Did she?

Lydia   Yeah, well, I mean, as I remember it, yes. Again, so what?

John   A few years back me and Tisha came over. We brought one of those platters with us.

Lydia   . . . and what? Me and your dad owe you sixty bucks for the food, son? Huh?

John   . . . we all sit down to eat and Pops is just gnawing at this damn rib. Just fighting with it. Yanking on it. Gotta mouth full of food and talks to us like we can understand him. But you understood him.

Lydia   Forty years of marriage will do that.

John   And he's squirming in his seat. You *deduce* that his foot is itching. So you jump up and go back to the room. You come out with some type of powder; some itch-shit. Gold Bond or whatever and you get on your hands and knees and start rubbing it into his foot. Right there at the dinner table. He's complaining the whole time that you ain't getting the right spot and you're on your hands and knees rubbing his fucking feet. At. The. Dinner. Table. And that's what made Tisha sick.

Lydia   . . .

John   Pops degraded you. He belittled you. He disregarded you. He was the worst husband I've ever witnessed. So, I separated him from that. He was whoever he was with you and with me he was the most profound, patient, wise motherfucker I ever knew. A wonderful, a beautiful father. And a God-forsaken husband. I extended that courtesy to him. I extended the same to you.

Lydia   You did no such thing. Ever. I would've loved you to. I'd have given my right arm for a little bit of grace from you.

John   Well, cut the damn thing off and send it to whoever it's owed. You wanna hear about grace? I was fourteen when you were going out of town to "visit Aunt Sherry." You were going to have to miss my track meet and felt bad about it, but I said hey, no big deal. Go be with sick ass Aunt Sherry. So, in trying to be . . . umm . . . I guess *sentimental* or some shit, I found your suitcase and stuck a picture of me and you from my last track meet in there. Lo and behold, lingerie, lesbian porn, and a goddamn dildo fall out the motherfucker. I was fourteen, woman! You don't think I had questions? You don't think I felt some kind of way? When I get on the computer and find your love letters to Scott and whoever the fuck else you met online, you think that's normal? But what happened when you came back in town? I greeted you, with open arms. I hugged you. Told you I missed you and listened to you bitch at me about my room not being clean. I knew then she's probably in a bad mood cause she had to say goodbye to her *lover* . . .

Lydia   My God, son . . .

John   Yeah, *my God*. (*Beat.*) That's grace. That's courtesy. Looking at you like a woman I could trust, that I could respect, that I could honor, all the while knowing what I knew—you owe me your right arm and every other limb you got. (*Beat.*) At least Pops wasn't so obtuse. He knew shit couldn't be hidden forever. He knew he owed me and Jazzy a little leniency. He knew when to say *alright, boy, you win this one. Do it your way.* But not you. You dug your heels in. You demanded a respect that doesn't exist. Do not grow, do not move, do not talk, do not think in a way you don't approve *for you are mother and next to God.*

Lydia   I never thought like that.

John   Bullshit.

Lydia   I carried those skeletons and couldn't eat or sleep or fucking breathe at times.

John   I saw you eating, sleeping, and breathing just fine.

Lydia   I'm telling you, son, you don't know . . .

John   You telling me what I know? After what I just said? You sure you want to do that? I know plenty.

Lydia   Jesus Christ, please . . . please, son. I . . . I thought I was doing the right thing. Regardless of my faults, still making sure I set expectations for you and your sister.

John   This ain't about expectations. You knew what you were up to and doubled down. You lost respect for yourself and tried to compensate for it by demanding more and more from me and Jazzy.

Lydia   . . . yeah, maybe that's what it was. Son, I was just so lonely. ⋀⋀⋀

John   So was I. ⋀⋀⋀

Lydia   You had friends and teammates. ⋀⋀⋀

John   I couldn't talk to them about this. ⋀⋀⋀

Lydia   But you could escape. ⋀⋀⋀

John   No, there wasn't an escape, Mama. ⋀⋀⋀

Lydia   I saw an opportunity to escape, too. ⋀⋀⋀

John   I said I didn't have no fucking escape! ⋀⋀⋀

Lydia   The things you found in that suitcase ⋀⋀⋀

John   Don't you tell me nothing about that shit! I ain't ask then and I ain't asking now!

Lydia   It's not what you think. They were fetish items. It wasn't for me.

John   Goddammit, Mama, I don't want to hear about that shit!

Lydia   I was empty, son. As cliché as it sounds.

John   Sounds cliché as hell.

Lydia   Every person requires a system. Support, encouragement, belief.

John   Every person requires a lot of things. And nobody gets it all. They don't go around with strap-ons in their back pocket looking for a good time.

Lydia   No, they have their own way of dealing with it.

John   With what?

Lydia   Feeling invisible. You and your sister had me and your father to support you. Your coaches to encourage you. Every damn body believed in you. I didn't have shit.

John   Sorry me and Jazzy were so damn inadequate.

Lydia   That's not what I'm saying at all, son. If it weren't for you and her I would've slit my wrists a long time ago. You two gave me a reason to keep living but I needed something to feel alive.

John   So, you're killing yourself with drugs to somehow feel alive? Where's the sense in that?

Lydia   No. The drugs are because I'm too afraid now to cut my wrists.

A moment.

John   You shouldn't say that type of shit.

Lydia   Why not? It doesn't scare you.

John   You're right, it doesn't.

Lydia   Of course, it doesn't.

John   Cause you ain't stupid enough to do something like that. You're fucked-up but you ain't that far gone. So don't sit here and act like you are.

Lydia   You don't know me. You do *not* know me. I don't know you. We aren't mother and son, we're perfect fucking strangers. So why say what one or the other is capable of doing?

John   You know what? We talked enough for today.

Lydia *looks at him and complies. She walks inside the house. He stands on the deck, trying his best to breathe out all the toxicity he just exposed himself to. His and his mother's fault. Suddenly and urgently,* **Lydia** *rushes back onto the patio. She has a razor in her hand and it's pressed against her wrist.*

Lydia   I told you if it weren't for you and your sister, I would've slit my goddamn wrists. Now that the both of you hate me / I might as well do it.

John   Mama, are you out your mind! Put that razor down. Stop fucking / around!

Lydia   Tell the truth! You hate / me don't you!

John   I'm going to call the police on your ass!

He's carefully trying to approach her but she moves around the table. He doesn't want to grab her. It's a bit of cat and mouse.

Lydia   Tell me you love me / or tell me you hate me! Pick one!

John   I'm asking you to just . . . fucking stop!

Lydia   Tell me the truth or lie to me and tell me you love me! I'll accept either one!

He's finally able to get to her and grabs her. He wraps her up. Her back is against his chest. She's bucking like a fucking wild bull. He has each wrist in one of his hands, preventing her from harming herself.

Lydia   Tell me! Say it! You fucking coward!

John   Mama, just stop! Please! Alright?! / Stop it!

Lydia   Say it! You hate me or you love me!

John   Mama!

Lydia   Well, I fucking hate you! You hear me? I fucking hate you!

He's wrestled the razor out of her hand. She's no longer a threat. He sits down looking out into nothing.

Lydia   Did you hear me? You hear what I said?

John   . . . Yeah. And I don't give a fuck.

Act Two

Scene One

John is on the patio, later that day, could be evening or night, director's choice. He's looking out. He walks out into the yard and pulls a couple weeds out the grass. He tosses them aside. He looks for something else to do. There isn't anything, but it's clear he doesn't want to go inside. Then, Tisha comes out onto the patio from inside the house. John walks back up to the patio to her.

John   She alright?

Tisha   . . . yeah.

John   Well . . . I um . . . I appreciate you coming over.

Tisha   Did I have a choice?

John   Ain't nobody drag you here.

Tisha   Well, Ms. Rita made it seem like you two were out here fighting to the death.

John   Ms. Rita needs to quit looking out them blinds all the damn time. I own my shit just like she owns her. She don't need to know what I'm doing over here.

Tisha   She's well within her right to report a disturbance.

John   Well, aren't you just *Ms. Civic-Fucking-Duty*. You don't talk this shit when you skip out on jury duty and help your mammy fuck over the tax man.

Tisha   Oh whatever, please.

John   Taking up for Ms. Rita. Hell, she the same one who called the cops when I was out here welding that fire pit. She don't think I know it but I do.

Tisha   It was midnight!

John   See, that shows how much you know. Doesn't matter what time it was. Welding don't make that much fucking noise, Tisha.

Tisha   It ain't quiet either!

John   I'm telling you I ain't wake her up. She was probably up anyways. She looks like a sad, reflective, miserable motherfucker. She was up walking around, looking, peeking, spying on a nigga and because she couldn't figure out what I was doing she called the cops. Nobody called the cops on her old funky ass when she was out here walking around with no panties on.

This tickles Tisha; this is something that gets kicked around often.

Tisha   Man, please! At least she had on a long nightgown. You must've been looking awfully hard to find out what she had going on way up there.

John   Nightgown? Nah, that slip—which is what it was, a *slip*—barely covered her damn labia.

Tisha   Jah-bo! Okay! Damn!

John   I'm saying, she bending over in broad daylight, acting like she looking at those flowers—that thing gonna hike up. I could've called the cops on her for indecent exposure or whatever. But instead, I chose to do the neighborly thing.

Tisha   Yeah, *neighborly*. Looking up that old woman's ass.

John   Why you gotta say it like that? Looking *up* it. Why can't you just say looking *at* it?

Tisha   At, up, in . . . whatever. A preposition is a preposition.

John   Man, fuck a preposition. I'm talking about just doing the decent thing.

Tisha   Which is?

John   Well, it ain't implying I been looking at Ms. Rita. (*Beat.*) And now, she wanna call you cause me and my mama out here talking.

Tisha   *Talking*?

John   Okay. Talking loud. Whatever.

Tisha   And damn near fighting.

John   I was trying to take a motherfucking razor out her hand!

Tisha   . . .

John   And I don't know why Ms. Rita calling you. You don't live here. Right?

Tisha   Jah-bo, I'm not about to do this with you. You know why I'm here. I'm not going to let you turn this into some *repartee* about me and you. Everything going on here and you wanna be opportunistic as fuck.

John   No repartee, huh? But you sure slid that last part in there.

Tisha   And rightfully so.

John   You think so?

A moment.

Tisha   You can't do this, you know? You can't let her stay here out of obligation.

John   She's my mother.

Tisha   I understand that.

John   I'm obligated to her.

Tisha   In some way, not like this though.

John   In what way then, Tisha?

Tisha   I don't know.

John   Sure you do. You must. Cause here you are making things *right again*. Pacifying her. Lecturing me. So just tell me because I ain't going to be able to figure it out. Teach me, Tisha. Make me a *learned* man.

Tisha   Why are you attacking me?

John   You come here and rub my back? Hug me? Touch my hand or something to let me know you give a fuck about whatever I may be feeling? Nah. You came and tucked my mama's ass in. Same woman who lied on you. Same woman who got between us and led us to where / we at now.

Tisha   No, no, no, ain't no blaming her. We're here because of us. She ain't help us by any means but she should've never been able to get between us. We shouldn't have let her.

John   You act like I put her there! I was willing to forget whoever and whatever she was to me. You said *no, that's your mother*. You told me to go kiss her. Wrap my arms around her. You said two years was too long to not talk to her and it was time to extend an olive branch. *What if something happens to her, how you gonna feel?* That's what you said. Well, I'll tell you how I'd feel—motherfucking free! Yeah that's my mama and I swear to God I love her. And I'd weep for her if something happened. A tear, maybe two but not no three or four. Fuck nah I ain't gonna stay up all night cradling myself asking what I'm supposed to do now and how am I supposed to do it. Nah, I ain't wondering that. Cause her love ain't shit. I been just fine without it. She ain't do me right. I went and opened up to her on your advice and she turned around and asked me for some money. Hadn't talked to her in two years and the moment I do she turns around and asks me for eighty-two dollars. Not eighty. Not eighty-five. Eighty-two with her crazy ass. And truth be told, you ain't do me right either. A lot of folks don't do me right. When I say I love a motherfucker you can tell. I don't waver. I don't back up people who ain't supposed to mean anything to me. I don't search for a principle that could justify why I don't have my people's back. Nah, I'll ride that ship to the bottom of the goddamn ocean. Right, wrong, otherwise. Cause I love you! But you take my mama's side, your mama's side, Ms. Rita, the damn black cat I shooed away, you'll take 'em all over me. You and everyone else. Sorry ass, worthless ass, fucking love.

She's hurt by this.

Tisha   I'm sorry you feel that way. (*Beat.*) Any and everything I do for that woman is really me doing for you. She hasn't been particularly charming in all the time I've known her. But she's running around with a razor so I try to calm her down. That's for you. So you don't have to try. I told you to go talk to her and hug her and kiss not because I felt she needed it but I was afraid of what you'd feel if you didn't and then something happened before you had the chance to do it.

John   It's unfortunate you're so concerned with so many things I'm not even concerned about. But the things I wanted you to notice, to care about, ain't none of that mean shit.

Tisha   I don't know why you're making this about us.

John   Because whenever it's you and me it's *us*. A hundred fucking years from now, if they bury me within earshot of you my goddamn skeleton gonna still be talking about *us*! Yeah I get it, you free and happy and at peace now. But I'm not. You standing here and I'd rather talk about us than my mama.

Tisha   Well, I wouldn't.

John   Then take your ass on! But I'm telling you what we gonna talk about as long as you standing here.

She begins to leave but turns back.

Tisha   You're a good man, Jah-bo. I know I didn't express that the way I should've. I know you didn't feel it as much as I wanted you to and that ain't nobody's fault but my own. But you're so damn calloused, baby. It takes a lot to get through to you. I tried, but you just didn't receive it. Not because you're ungrateful, but you're hurt. And you thought you could heal on your own. And I thought I could help you heal. But I just got to a point where I had to accept my own limitations. I can't. I was never going to be able to make you feel as loved as you were. I can't spend the rest of my life with a daily reminder of how inadequate my love is. Maybe it is, but I don't want the reminder.

John   I never implied you were inadequate. In any way.

Tisha   You implied I'm just like your mama and incapable of standing with you when you need it most. That I'd rather carry that black cat around. That's what you said. Ain't it?

John   I was just talking.

Tisha   But you can't always *just talk*. You can't just say whatever and do whatever and think somebody supposed to know what you really mean. Nah, you never called me out my name. *Bitch* ain't ever been on your lips or in your eyes when you were talking to me and I appreciate that. Instead you called me useless /

John   / I ain't ever said no shit like that!

Tisha   by implying anything that I do for you ain't what you really need. That /

John   / That ain't what I was saying.

Tisha   all the things you need I don't ever do. You / imply

John   / I'm telling you that ain't what I was saying.

Tisha   that my love and my indifference feels the same way. And that ain't the fucking definition of inadequacy? Uselessness?

John   . . .

Tisha   Maybe that's why your mother shouldn't be here. She'll never be able to convince you she loves you. You'll never convince her. You'll be two people sitting here out of an obligation you can't even explain. Obligation without love is a prison. It's doing time. A helping hand without any love is patronizing. That's what you and your mama have here and that's what we ended up with.

John   I love you, Tisha. And I never said you ain't love me, I just said the shit ain't feel how I needed it to.

Tisha   You act like your love feels so damn good all the time. That you know how to give it and show it in a way that leaves everyone better than what you found them and all they gotta do is sit back and receive it. You think if everyone just learned how to love the way you did this whole damn world would be saved. But you still got some shit to learn too, Jah-bo. About love. About grace. About reciprocation. Your expectations, man—it's the heaviest fucking thing I ever had to carry. And you put them on everyone, talking about how you carry all of their expectations right back. But you don't, baby. You try, but you drop a lot of shit along the way. Shit that might not mean anything to you but means everything to someone else. It falls and you just keep on going, patting yourself on the back for all the things you still carrying. But that shit you dropped was important. Patience, tolerance, being able to break the ice. How you think it feels to know you love me but can go weeks without talking to me because you're mad? I gotta come crawling to you every time. How does that exist in the same space as love? (*Beat.*) Now, you can blame whatever you don't know on your mama and daddy. You can say you had to learn it all on your own; don't change the fact that no matter how good it feels—and it does, it feels so good sometimes, to be loved by you—it still comes at a cost. Yeah, you give folks their flowers, but your roses got thorns in 'em too. And it fucking hurts sometimes, Jah-bo. Man, the shit can scratch and scrape and cut and you think it's okay because of how good it feels when it don't. They need a Band-Aid but you saying *nah, don't it smell good though?* But it's hard to think about how pretty the fucking rose smells when you're sitting there bleeding.

This hits him. Maybe hurts him.

John   I took a long, hard look at myself years ago. I was dumb-young. Wasn't nobody else around me being that introspective nor reflective. Or maybe they were and I just didn't know it like they didn't know it about me. We were just some little niggas ripping and running, but in closed spaces I thought about shit. I caught myself thinking about what the fuck am I going to become. I was looking at my daddy and my mama and knew it was inevitable—I was going to be fucked-up.

Tisha   You ain't fucked-up. You're flawed. I'm flawed. We're all crooked trying to get straight.

John   Some of us mighty crooked then, I guess. I had always hoped, though, me not doing some of the things my daddy did and some of the things my mama did—the worst things—would be enough. That I could cancel out the shit I did do with good things. But to hear you tell it, and I know you're right, it just don't work that way. But I never tried to trick you. Or imply I ain't have my ways about me. I wasn't even trying to hide it from you. I just knew I was fucked-up and hoped you didn't know it too.

Tisha   I want you to do me a favor. Okay?

John   . . . of course.

Tisha   Don't be impenetrable. How you know to pull away or stop when something is hurting you if you don't let yourself feel it?

John   I ain't hurting. Maybe at one time I was. But I ain't hurt. If I was, I'd say it.

Tisha   No you wouldn't.

John   Why wouldn't I? I ain't never said I was the baddest motherfucker there ever was.

Tisha   Well . . . tell me that it hurts.

John   What hurts? I don't know what you're talking about. I'm mad. I'm frustrated. My mama is fucking up. I can look back and be upset with my old man too. I'm mad you quit on me but I get it. That said I ain't hurt. Shit, this is life.

Tisha   . . . I didn't quit on you.

John   Well, whatever it was. I already said you were justified. I ain't blaming you. Still, we could've kept going, you said no. That's quitting.

She holds his face in her hand, tenderly.

Tisha   Baby, you're hurt. And until you admit that, you ain't gonna be able to fix the shit that's hurting you. You can't fix your mama. You can't save her until you forgive her. You can't forgive her until you learn to love her again.

John   I ain't ever stopped loving my mama.

Tisha   Then forgive her. Forgive her knowing she may never change. And that ain't easy. And I ain't saying that even I'd be able to do it. But I ain't you. You're built for it.

She kisses him and starts to leave.

John   Forgive *me* then . . . why can't you do that? You forgive me. I'll forgive her. She can keep doing whatever she doing but I can be better, baby. Shit can start to make sense again.

Tisha   I have, Jah-bo . . .

She leaves. **John** *meanders about for a moment and then* **Lydia** *comes out to the patio.*

Lydia   Did Tisha leave?

John   She just did.

Lydia   Damn. Alright.

John   Whatchu need?

Lydia   Nothing. I was just going to ask her to take me to get some cigarettes and something to eat.

John   I can take you. Or just go get it for you. Whichever.

Lydia   No. That's alright.

John   I can take you to get some food, Mama.

Lydia   I'll be fine. I'll eat whatever's in there. I just wanted to get out for a bit. I don't suppose *you* want to drive me around.

John   . . .

Lydia   Didn't think so.

John   You think Tisha does?

Lydia   No. But she's a better actor than you. She lets me think she doesn't mind. So, I act too, right along with her. But I'm not dumb. I know she hates me.

John *looks at his mother. Something occurs to him. He laughs to himself, slightly.*

John   You laugh. I say I'm hated and you laugh. Help me see the funny, son.

John   It's just . . . I finally see what it feels like, to keep hearing someone say that shit. How unloved and mistreated they are. Tisha says I do it too. No wonder she's gone. (*Beat.*) Yeah, this might be the first time I ever looked at you and saw me. Or looked at myself and saw you. Either way, I'm seeing some common ground. Something we're getting from each other.

Lydia   Well, you came from me so you got from me; I ain't get nothing from you but a stretched-out womb from carrying you a month too long.

He replies with sincerity, not malice nor aggression.

John   And what did I get from you, Mama?

Lydia   Oh no, no, no. No thank you. I don't want to play this game.

John   No, Mama, I'm asking sincerely. I'm your son, aren't I?

Lydia   You most certainly are.

John   And you're my mother?

Lydia   I've been here for every day of your life plus another nine months, three weeks and twenty-two hours that I carried you and fought like hell to push you out. I'm the only mother you got.

John   Then I'm asking, where's your proof? When you standing there looking at me, what proof you got?

Lydia   . . . *proof?* I gave up a long time ago on hoping anyone would see something between us. I see a little bit of me in your face but I know you don't wanna own up to that. Nobody else sees it. Maybe it's just wishful thinking but I think you do look a little like me. But not enough to prove anything. Instead, I just think about all the things you keep to yourself.

John   What things?

Lydia   Some years ago, this was before you or your sister were born, your dad wanted to take me down to Alabama to meet his family. We drive down there, it's about a nine-hour trip, and the entire time he's prepping me. He tells me everyone in his family are big talkers. Tells me not to talk over them but don't just let them talk over me either or they will. *Find some sweet spots*—he said. Well, there weren't no sweet spots. I was there two days and might've said five words. On the third day, your father, his dad, and me go out to get something to eat. Your grandpa was the biggest talker of them all. And what made it worse was he could never stay focused on any one thing. He'd talk about something at his job and cut himself off to talk about a dog he might see. That dog would remind him of something else and he'd get on that and then lose his train of thought. Before long he's just rambling. After about forty minutes, we're in the car and he looks back at me and says *how come you don't ever have much to say, sweetheart?* I looked at him and I mean looked right at him without any hesitation and said *because you already said it all*. That tickled the shit out of your grandpa. He goes *well, I'll tell you this, whenever you do say something it looks like you say too damn much.* That was a charming ass man. Like your dad. Like you. You get that from them. You get your smarts from your big sister. She'd come home and teach you everything she learned and so you were always ahead of the curve. But not feeling like you always have to talk, not always revealing your hand but instead waiting—waiting for when it'll matter the most, you get that from me. People always talk about what you see is what you get and that's fine too. But what about saving a little something for later? And I miss that. I miss being hard to figure out. Now, I'm just worn and torn and probably bitter and nobody second guesses it.

John   I'm not sure I'm as reserved as you think I am.

Lydia   You used to be. Maybe you've outgrown it. It's how I see you still. (*Beat.*) I got the right to do that sometimes. Look at you and still see my baby boy.

John   . . .

Lydia   Or maybe I don't, I don't know. (*Beat.*) So I don't know you at all?

John   I'm not saying that. I guess I'm somewhat introverted. That's not something I would've attributed to you though.

Lydia   Well, I tried to give you things, son.

John   You did. You gave me something better than that though.

Lydia   I can't wait to hear this.

John   Nah, it's actually . . . well, you gave me something vital, Mama. (*Beat.*) I was in the second grade and you came to pick me up from school. I started to walk to you and I guess you heard a few of the kids ask me *is that your mama?* And they laughed. The shit was funny to them. Didn't bother me but I guess you wanted to make sure it never did. So, we get in the car and you asked me *do kids ever ask you what you are?* I'm thinking shit, I know my hair is long and curly but it ain't that damn long. People know I'm a boy. Damn sure a person. I must've made a face . . . do you remember this?

Lydia   Not really.

John   Well, you wanted to know if folks asked me if I'm Black or white or what. So, I told you yeah they ask sometimes and I just tell them I'm mixed.

Lydia   Yeah . . . yeah, I remember this.

John   And you said no, I ain't mixed. I'm Black. My daddy's Black and so am I. I just happen to have a white mama. And that was the day couldn't nobody tell me shit about who or what I was ever again. I was Black. I was a man. Or I was gonna be someday. I belonged to God. I was my daddy's son and my mama's baby. None of that shit was up for negotiation. You gave me that, Mama. I've never been afraid to be who I was and I've never hesitated to define what that meant. If my white mama is telling me I'm beautiful and Black and not even her blood is enough to water that down, what the fuck can anybody else say about it?

Lydia   Honestly, I can't remember what my reasoning was at the time. I guess I didn't want you to feel *different*. Black was the only thing you could be looking how you look. You sure took it and ran with it. Ran as far away from me as you could.

John   Why would you say something like that?

Lydia   Seems like you went out your way to prove things about yourself. And I can get you trying to prove it to the world but why'd you have to prove it to me? You took your shots, son, every chance you got. To make sure I knew we weren't nothing alike.

John   I wasn't proving anything. Everything I am ain't because of you or simply to spite you. Some of this is just me. Some shit I figured out on my own. I mean damn, Mama, how much you want us to have in common? You think you're that *grand* of a person? You ain't got enough awareness to see how diseased you are and want better for me?

Lydia   Diseased? Well there's a new one.

John *takes a moment; he's trying to just talk to her.*

John   The worst I ever heard you and Pops getting into it was a week before Christmas when I was in the third grade. I remember because that was the year you all got me and Jazzy so much shit. Every single thing I asked for I got and I didn't ask for nothing small. I got a go-kart, a pool table, you got us a computer to share, Jazzy got a camcorder and you had been wanting one of those for yourself. Then on top of that we got tons of clothes. The clothes didn't mean that much to me, but I knew it was a lot.

Lydia   We always did that for Christmas.

John   No, this year was different. I always figured it was you all trying to make us remember that Christmas in a different way. Instead, I always think about the fight just a week before. I remember you both wishing death on each other. Hadn't heard y'all say that before. I heard shit getting knocked over. I buried myself under my blankets and pillows trying to mute everything. But you were too loud. Then I hear this thick gurgling noise; this gasp and it was the only sound left. I just started praying

God, let my mama be alright. I knew it wasn't him making that noise. I knew it was him choking you. And once he let you go you threw a knife at him and sliced him good. And I felt like such a bitch. Such a coward. My mama could've been hurt and I laid in my bed, tucked under blankets and fucking stuffed animals hoping it would all go away. And it put something in me, Mama. I said *never again.* I won't ever feel like no coward again. If someone looked at me wrong, I'd fight 'em. If they said something to me I ain't like, I'd fight 'em. If they called you a white bitch I'd try to kill 'em. Sometimes pops would pick me up from school and he'd have on his overalls and work boots and they'd say something about him, I'd try to kill them too. I learned to hate people and it didn't take much to flip that switch. Fast forward a few years later, I was fifteen and this kid took my bike when I wasn't looking. He brought it back but I still ain't appreciate he took it to begin with. Had me out there looking for it. After a while, he finally came back with it. I ran up on him so fast and I knocked his ass off that bike and started kicking him in his head. I don't know, maybe eight or nine times. His head got pinned against a cinder block propping up the porch. Ms. Kendra tried to pull me off but I kicked him in the head that one last time.

Lydia   Jesus, son, I know this story. We don't have to relieve it.

John   Nah, you know I damn near killed some kid. You know I had to get therapy. That I missed a year of school while in juvenile. You know that you and Pops stood back and act confused about it all, put on the performance of a lifetime so they didn't take me from y'all. *Had to be a chemical imbalance. Had to be the hood that exposed me to too much.* Right? I had to take pills I didn't even fucking need. You know Pops sends that kid's mother a thousand bucks a month still because the little nigga could never walk again or talk right.

He is getting emotional, he hates himself for this.

You know we don't ever talk about it. Just swept it under the rug. But you don't know that I still see him every now and then. At the store, I'll see his mama pushing him around in his wheelchair. And she's a God-fearing woman so she politely nods and I'll help her put her bags in the car if we leave at the same time. But that ain't for her. She lets me do that for me. Because otherwise I got all this goddamn guilt crushing me. How I get to ever have anything normal in my life when he has to live the way he does? Because I had good grades and he didn't. Because he had a little rap sheet and I didn't. I came from a two-parent home and he didn't. So oh well, give me a few pills and a few sessions and set me back a year in school. That should set shit right because, after all, what good was that little nigga really gonna be?! And you know what else you don't know, when it all gets too heavy for me, I tell myself *well, he shouldn't have taken my bike.*

Lydia   You—you—you made a mistake, son. He made one. You made one. Had you toppled over it could've been me pushing you around in a wheelchair.

John   And would you be kind to him, Mama? Let him help you with your bags? Huh? Nah, you wouldn't. Because we don't have that in us. We hate people. And we hate each other.

Lydia   I don't hate nobody.

John   ... Pops came to visit me one day in juvey. Was just us. And he told me, *son, I've told you and showed you too much. Too much about me. Things you hear me say to your mother you don't ever need to say to no woman. Things you see me do, you don't ever need to do. The way you see me with other folks, that's what enabled you to jump on that kid. But I don't want this for you. You hear me, boy? I. Don't. Want. This. For. You. I DON'T WANT THIS SHIT FOR YOU! I got some good things in me to offer you, boy, but I'd rather you reject it all if it it'll make sure you miss getting the bad parts of me. Just go another way. Be like someone else. Anyone else. Because you gotta be better than me. You got to. God ain't gonna show me no grace if you ain't because He blessed me with self-awareness. He gave me that. So I can make sure you better than me and if I don't make sure of at least that, if you end up like me, I know I'm going to hell twice.* That's what he said. (*Beat.*) I say all this to ask you, Mama, knowing yourself and what you exposed me and Jazzy to, can you understand why I went another way? Pops does. Can you? Can you see why being like you was the last thing I ever wanted to be? Why having a woman like you was the last thing in this world I ever wanted?

Lydia   So I poisoned you and ruined you and now here we are. Despite all of that, you're trying to *save me*? Is that what it is? Is this going to make that kid walk again?

John   / Nah, I'm gonna answer for that still.

Lydia   I've never given you or done anything good for you, still you're willing to bring your old useless mother in and fix her all the while reminding me of just how fucking little I mean to you?

John   That's the shit Tisha was talking about. I get that from you too. Somebody loves me the best they can and because it ain't how I want it I tell them it ain't shit. What they say they see in me don't matter because it ain't what I want them to see. So I just stomp around feeling sorry for myself. You gave me that too. (*Beat.*) I told you what you did for me. I told you that you planted that seed of belonging and self-worth. But that ain't good enough for you.

Lydia   Big fucking deal, son! I told you that you were Black. So what? Any goddamn mirror would've told you the same thing.

John   Well, it meant something to me. It emboldened me. It made me feel like I had the right to be me.

Lydia   And who are you, son?

John   You won't ever know, Mama.

Lydia   But let me guess, Tisha knows, right?

John   I don't know what in the world would make you bring her up to me; especially if you trying to compare you and her. You won't ever compare to her.

Lydia   You brought her up.

John   I was just saying what she helped me see in myself.

Lydia   As it relates to me. That I somehow taught you to feel sorry for yourself.

John   Yeah that's pretty accurate.

Lydia   She helped you see so much but she still left your sorry ass.

John   It ain't over yet. I gotta chance still. She might end up mine again.

Lydia   How? Getting me out the way? You wanna blame me for you and her too?

John   Nah. I'll take the blame for this one. Although you lying on her ain't help none. Begging Pops for money, talking about Tisha begging you for it because we need money and I'm too prideful to ask. All that just so you can get some drugs.

Lydia   . . .

John   Oh what's that? Is that shame? Is that embarrassment? Regret? What is that on your face, woman? Why you so quiet all of a sudden?

Lydia   Yes goddammit! / I'm ashamed!

John   And don't get me wrong. I'm angry with Pops about it too. He should've known better. But it was just easier for him to believe you.

Lydia   Goddammit I said I'm sorry!

John   Did you? When? You ain't say that to me. You tell her? Huh? Nah, I know you haven't or she would've told me. You just want it to go away. You want to ask her for favors with your old, senile, entitled ass. But I know for a fact you ain't ever said sorry. Why is that?

Lydia   . . .

John   Waiting for the perfect time? Well, hell, no time better than the present. Here you go . . .

He grabs his cellphone from his pocket or wherever he may have laid it down on the patio.

Call her now. Tell her how ashamed and sorry you are. If you're truly sorry.

He offers the phone but she doesn't take it.

Here, I'll dial.

He goes through his phone and she slaps it out his hand.

Lydia   Go fuck yourself! (*Beat.*) If me and your father are who you say we are, if you knew what she'd be up against and you still threw her right in the middle of it, all of our shit and your shit too, son—then guess what? You are to fucking blame! Not me.

John   And I own that.

Lydia   Yeah, I lied. I lied and I lied and I lied. But that woman wouldn't have left you because of that. No. So what did you do to make her leave? How much of your dad do you have in you?

John   Not nearly as much as you'd like to think.

Lydia   You rough her up a little?

John   Not a single fucking time.

Lydia   How many *bitches* has she been?

John   I ain't going to play this game with you, Mama.

Lydia   Oooh, so that's what it was?

John   You might want to calm down.

Lydia   I didn't hear you deny it.

John   I ain't never call her out her name.

Lydia   So you stepped out on her? Came home smelling like some other woman and tried to throw her off the scent by bitching about something she might've done.

John   Nah.

Lydia   Yeah you did!

John   I ain't going to keep telling you to calm your ass down.

Lydia   Because if none of that then what you're telling me is you're just one sorry ass man. Who you got to blame for that, son? You're so enlightened. *One with yourself.* You got it all figured out and you still chose to be unbearable?

John   You know the difference between me and you?

Lydia   Besides the fifty million things you've already told me about? No, what is it, *brotherman*?

John   You're the type of person to stab someone in their back and say, well, at least I didn't shoot you in the head. But see, you and Pops set the bar too low. All that sick ass shit between you and him never made it into my marriage, but that don't make me a great husband. I looked at her one day and realized she felt unseen and unheard and she wasn't accustomed to feeling like that. I didn't want to be the one to introduce her to it. I suffocated her with all my sad stories until her only purpose became trying to make shit better that she couldn't. So when she left, and I ain't want her to, I can't even say I let her, I just got out the way.

Lydia   Why not just change?

John   Are you out your damn mind, woman? Who am I to trick someone into staying with me? Expecting them to just stick with me while I figure shit out. Hustling them. Bamboozling them. Promising things I'm not sure I can give. Don't you understand that I don't expect shit from people like you do? Ol' lying ass woman! Thieving ass woman! Selfish ass woman! Drug addict ass woman!

She gets emotional.

Lydia   So that's what this is about? Me expecting my family to stand by me when I need it most? My kids? My husband? I'm fucking sick, son! And you want me to just go out there and roll over and die! By myself!

John   I want you to change!

Lydia   I'm trying!

John   No you ain't.

Lydia   Goddamn you!

John   How many pills you pop today?

Lydia   I'm calling your father.

John   Call him. Go back to him and wear him down. Be a burden. Until he goes to sleep one day and don't wake back up. Because better him than you, right? Better me than you, right? Jazzy? You got the right to live even if it means destroying everything around you.

Lydia   You little son of a bitch! I had the razor didn't I?! Didn't I? And you took it from me. That's alright. I'm going to do it one day. I'm going to cut my damn wrists off and I want you to know you put the razor in my hands!

John   Your ass needs to be in a padded room, you know that?

Lydia   Why, so you can complain about how much it costs?

John   I'll gladly pay that. It'd be the investment of a lifetime. And I might even come and feed you your soup every now and then. But we both know you wouldn't go.

Lydia   You don't know what I'm capable of.

John   You never cease to amaze me, that's for sure.

Lydia   Well, maybe I got another trick for you then, you little bastard.

John   Nah, you ain't got shit for me. Anything you do anymore is only for you, Mama.

Lydia   Tell me what you want then, son? You brought me here. I came. I stayed. But everything you're saying tells me you don't want me here. So just say it?

John   . . .

Lydia   Want me to go out there and die?

John   Don't do this shit, Mama.

Lydia   Just tell me. You want me here or you want me gone? You want me safe or you want me dead? Either you love me or you hate me. Tell me.

John   I showed you.

Lydia   You haven't shown me shit! Oh what? Grabbing that razor from me? Any human being would've done that. What have you shown me as a son, though?

John   I guess nothing. What am I supposed to show someone who hates me? Remember that? Ain't that what you said?

She stares him down. She looks away in shame. She takes a moment.

Lydia   Alright then. Well, let me show you how I really feel about you then. What mama is willing to do for her boy.

She goes inside. **John** *stands outside. Then it occurs to him what she could possibly be talking about. With great urgency and panic he runs inside while yelling for her.*

John   Mama!

While inside we hear tussling and struggle; she grunts and yells.

Damnit it woman, will you just stop?! Mama, give it to me!

Lydia   Let me go goddammit! Let me show you! I'll show you and your dad and your sister! Damn you!

Finally, the struggle has stopped, and she weeps loudly, inconsolably. He comes back out onto the patio and tosses a small sharp knife presumably he took from his mother. He sits in silence. A few moments pass and she comes out but keeps her distance. She stands behind him. Broken. She begins to sing a song; it's all she can do to push it out but he recognizes it.

Lydia
>   And when you've grown, can hold your own
>   I'll be there to help you hold it still
>   And time will tell if I'll grow frail
>   You'll be there for me; I know you will . . .

John *then joins in and sings a single line with her, never looking at her. This is familiar to them both, maybe something from so long ago.*

John/Lydia
>   I know you will, your baby boy
>   You know I will . . .

LYDIA   I love you. You hear me? I love you, son . . .

He never replies nor acknowledges her.

The end.